The Imperial Cities
of Morocco

The Imperial Cities of Morocco

MOHAMED MÉTALSI
CÉCILE TRÉAL
JEAN-MICHEL RUIZ

| Cover illustration
MAUSOLEUM OF THE SAADIAN PRINCES
The *mihrab*, the niche indicating
the direction of Mecca, is richly
decorated with stucco-work.
On the floor of the mausoleum
the tombs of members of the
princes' families are indicated
by rectangles of coloured *zillij*.

| Page 2
BOU INANIA MEDRASA, FEZ
The walls of the inner courtyard
are richly carved. The opening,
ornamented with interlacing designs
and stalactites of chiselled plaster,
rests on a console of carved wood.

Editor: Geneviève Rudolf
Translation: Mark Hutchinson
Copy editing: Jack Liesveld
Art design: Marthe Lauffray
Cover design: Laurent Gudin
Map design: Béatrice Garnier
Filmsetting and lithography: Litho Service, Verona

Published with the assistance of the French Ministry
responsible for Culture, Centre National du Livre
© FINEST SA / EDITION PIERRE TERRAIL, PARIS 1999
© English edition, 2000
ISBN: 2-87939-224-1
Publication number: 277
Printed in Italy

AL ATTARIN MADRASA, FEZ (DETAIL)
A harmonious combination
of the three main motifs
of Arabo-Moslem ornamentation:
geometrical forms,
vegetal arabesques and
cursive calligraphy.

Page 6 |
MENARA PAVILION, MARRAKESH
The pavilion was built by
Saadian sultans and modified
in the nineteenth century.
The huge artificial reflecting pool
was built in the twelfth century
by Almohad sovereigns.

Contents

The Dynastic Legacy

Few countries enjoy a geographical situation as exceptional as that of Morocco, which lies on the edge of two seas and two continents. The sheer vastness of the Atlantic Ocean, "Mother of Darkness" as Arab geographers called her, made Morocco the furthermost tip of the known world prior to the discovery of America. It is also the westernmost country of the Moslem world, whence its Arab name, *d'al Maghrib al Aqsa* ("the land of the setting sun" or "the far west"). At the same time Mediterranean, Atlantic, Saharan and Western, Morocco is a mosaic of peoples and cultures, and, on account of its strategic position, came within the sphere of influence of the great Mediterranean civilisations as long ago as antiquity. In the twelfth century BC, the Phoenicians set up trading posts in Tingis, Tamuda, and later in Lixus. Carthaginian settlers continued until the second century BC, while, inland, the Berber tribes united to found the Kingdom of Mauritania. In AD 40, the Romans annexed part of Morocco, which became Mauritania Tingitana, a province that took part in the main economic and cultural exchanges engendered by the Roman Empire. The Roman presence resulted mainly in the founding of settlements such as Volubilis, Lixus and Tingis, and in the colonisation of the countryside. It was the Byzantines who brought to a close the long period of antiquity by taking possession of the fortified towns of Tangier and Ceuta. By the time the Moslems arrived, Morocco was to all intents and purposes a rural territory.

The Moslem conquest of the Maghrib in the late seventh century is the most important single event in Morocco's history. A new form of civilisation replaced the Latin and Christian influences, integrating the country with the Arabo-Moslem world. In foisting itself on the conquered populations, Islam, which was endowed with a rare force of conviction, made possible the flowering of a communal culture and a federative state. In this way arose the first of the six great dynasties that were to follow one another without interruption for twelve hundred years.

The Idrissids were the founders of the first Islamic state in Morocco. From the eleventh to the thirteenth centuries, the Almoravids and the Almohads, Berber dynasties that had converted to Islam, built the great Ibero-Maghribin empire which at its height extended across the whole of North Africa and northwards into Andalusia. The Merinids, who ruled over Morocco from the thirteenth century, did their utmost to restore order and unity to the Maghrib, which was subject to Christian incursions, and

THE RUINS OF VOLUBILIS

Founded by the Berbers and later occupied by the Carthaginians, the town became the capital of the Roman province of Mauritania Tingitana in 40 BC. The Moslems took possession of the town at the end of the eighth century.

created a brilliant urban civilisation. The attitude adopted by the final dynasties – the Saadian dynasty between the sixteenth and seventeenth centuries, followed by the Alouite dynasty of Hassan II and Mohammed IV – was above all defensive, but, though they managed to prevent the country being overrun by the Portuguese and Spanish, Morocco finally fell into a long period of decline that would culminate, after all kinds of political and military adventures, in occupation by France and Spain. It wasn't until 1956 that an end was put to the French and Spanish Protectorates signed in 1912.

"For a great king, a great city", wrote the famous Maghribin historian, Ibn Khaldoun, in the fourteenth century. The imperial capitals are clearly the legacy of those dynasties. Their conquering kings, whose authority extended over a vast, thriving territory, were anxious to see the influence they exercised engraved in stone. When a Moroccan dynasty decided to take up residence in Fez, Marrakesh, Rabat or Meknes, the city, henceforth a capital ('asima), would adorn itself with palaces, mosques and mausoleums testifying to the prince's prestige in the eyes of his contemporaries and of history. Such was the majesty, sophistication and luxury of the royal city that, in the minds of medieval authors, it became a mythical universe which conjured up images drawn from legend.

The presence of the royal court in a city determines the monumental proportions of its buildings, the perfection of its architecture and art and, finally, its size. As the focus both of the king's official life, with its receptions and ceremonies, and of his private life, it must embody the finest architectural achievements of its day.

The Urban Heritage

The four imperial cities of Morocco are all laid out in the same way, displaying a tightly-knit urban structure hemmed round by ramparts flanked with watchtowers and fortifications. Cutting through the tangle of narrow streets are a series of main roads connecting the gates of the city to one another, along with a few more or less median roads, their existence constantly under threat from the houses and walls that jut out above the streets.

For all the apparent disorder, the construction of these cities is governed by strictly logical imperatives: the exterior aspects of the kasbah (the citadel of the prince), the central position of the great mosque, religious and ethnic segregation, differentiation of commercial and residential areas, and the siting of activities according to how much pollution they generate.

The hierarchy according to which the streets are organized gives the plan a distinctive shape, from the all but rectilinear main arteries and the narrow streets giving access to the different districts, to the tiny private residential streets which isolate the houses, protecting them from the gaze of outsiders. The narrow streets form a spider's web linking the inside to the outside world and to all the main centres of exchange and communication. The medina, the historic city, is an area open to circulation, therefore, its favoured sites are the great mosque (or mosques, when there is more than one), the souks and the kasbah. At the same time, bounded by walls fitted with gates placed at wide intervals from one another, the medina is

MINARET OF A MADRASA, FEZ
Most Moroccan minarets are
of a Hispano-Mauresque type,
a square tower usually built
at the corner of the sanctuary.

MEDINA OF MARRAKESH
This aerial view gives a good
idea of the tightly-knit
structure of Moslem towns,
the interlocking buildings
all but obscuring the network
of narrow streets and alleys.

sometimes closed at night and, by filtering entrance, can be used as an instrument of exclusion.

A variety of customary regulations determine where activities are located within the kasbah. Contrasting with the silent, deserted alleys and dead-end streets are the streets packed with noisy crowds pouring into the souks to buy and sell. The commercial district of the medina is a tangle of little shops, storehouses and semi-rural souks arranged in a hierarchy that spreads outwards from the centre to the ramparts. The order is determined by two criteria: a subjective criteria, which takes into account the value of the products on offer according to their manufactured quality and degree of transformation; and a criteria of commodity, the one being not unconnected with the other. Polluting activities are often located near appropriate spots (water points, for example) and away from the centre, whereas manufacturers and purveyors of luxury goods are established near the mosque. This being said, there are very few fixed models of this kind; a great many markets and professions have ceased to exist, moved elsewhere or been scattered about the city. The culminating point of this arrangement is the *kissariya*. Traditionally found at the centre, the *kissariya* consists of a group of buildings basically regular in design (as in Fez) and is traversed by parallel streets that intersect with one another at right angles, the outlets of which are fitted with gates that are locked at night. Tradesman are also grouped together there according to the type of produce they offer for sale.

STREETS IN THE FEZ MEDINA
Far from the bustle of the souks, the streets leading to private houses are used only by residents. In this maze of narrow streets you often end up in a blind alley.

FONDOUKS
Used as inns, warehouses or workshops, *fondouks* play an important part in the organization of the souks. The two-storied Sagha *Fondouk* in Fez was used by goldsmiths.

Economic activities – apart from industrial establishments such as flour-mills, oil factories, cloth mills and tanneries – occupy buildings of one of two kinds. The first kind is the *hanut* or shop, the main form of business premises for craftsmen and tradesmen. The *hanut* has hardly changed since the Middle Ages and consists of a small rectangular or square room of varying size that is generally easy and cheap to build, making it easy to create new souks merely by placing one shop next to another. The second kind is the *fondouk* or caravanserai, an all-purpose building sometimes used to house caravans and travellers (tradesmen or pilgrims, along with their beasts of burden), sometimes to store wholesale merchandise waiting to be sold or to go up for auction. The *fondouk* usually takes the form of a large rectangular or square building of one or two storeys organized around a large open courtyard surrounded by porticoes and at the centre of which a fountain is sometimes found. Shops are located on the ground floor, the rooms on the upper floor (or floors) being reserved for living quarters.

In a hot country, the distribution of water is a particularly crucial factor in the life and organization of a city. In Marrakesh, Morocco's southern metropolis situated at the gateway to the pre-Saharan valleys, a network of underground pipes has been installed to supply its mosques, houses and fountains with water. The importance attached to water in the city can also be explained by the recommendations of the Koran, which require that water be offered to the thirsty. As early as the Almohad period, cities were

Built by wealthy patrons, mural fountains enliven the monochrome walls of Moroccan medinas with their brightly coloured compositions. The imperial cities have some famous ones: Al Nejjarin in Fez, Dar Jamai in Meknes, Chrob in Marrakesh.

DAR SI SAID PALACE, MARRAKESH
The *riad*, the garden found in the more well-to-do homes, is often laid out in the Andalusian style, with raised paths surrounding the flower-beds.

AERIAL VIEW OF A TRADITIONAL HOUSE
The self-contained household gives onto two large open-air areas. In the larger of the two, surrounded by a gallery, a garden has been laid out.

furnished with dozens of water points. Fez had eighty; princes and rich merchants built large numbers of them. In all the imperial cities lavishly decorated public fountains (*seqqaya*) decorate the streets and souks. Their appearance has not changed over the centuries. They usually consist of an oblong basin, of varying size, set into a wall and delicately ornamented with polychrome *zillij*.

Far from the souks, narrow winding streets (some of them covered) are reserved for the inhabitants of the city; visitors from the countryside or from abroad will only set foot there in connection with family or business matters. In the not too distant past, the districts formed relatively autonomous entities and were sometimes sealed off behind gates, like most of the districts in the medinas of Fez and Marrakesh. That is why certain everyday necessities – ovens (*ferrane*), *hammams*, Koranic colleges (*msid*), grocery shops (*baqqal*) – can be found there. On the other hand, there is no trade in luxury goods in the neighbourhood. This semi-cloistered life-style does not prevent the inhabitants from merging with the larger network of the city as a whole. Important purchases or praying in the Great Mosque are ways of expressing one's membership in that community, and the ritual practices in which the population collectively indulges once a year on the anniversary of the Prophet's birth are a sign of this. During the festivities, neighbourhood organizations, corporations and brotherhoods come together from all over the medina to celebrate the patron saints of the town, manifesting the unity of the city in this way.

The Great Mosque has supreme control over all the city's activities: it is a place of worship, a university, a law court, a sanctuary and a place of conviviality where nothing must come in the way of one's duties towards God and one's fellow men. The social and urban symbol of an authority that impresses itself upon the mind, the minaret, looking down over the city, sums up the ethics of the city-dweller's life. The call to prayer, sounded five times a day by the *muezzin*, punctuates the flow of the day and serves as a reminder of the unity of the Moslem community.

The residential sector, on the other hand, would seem to make it all but impossible to pass from one place to another. Joined by a network of narrow streets, each block is a tightly–knit unit of one-or two-storey houses separated by blind alleys in which further dwellings are hidden away. An essential part of the city, the blind alley, far from being the result of some anarchic growth, is the natural culmination of streets that branch off from the main thoroughfare. It is here that realities which go unnoticed by the casual visitor but which extend over the greater part of the city's surface are concealed. Barred to strangers, this particular city, hidden away within its sacred enclosure, is not designed as a place to stroll in. Its function is to uphold the separation between public and private space, and by extension, between the lives of men and the secret, closely-guarded world of women.

Houses are designed in accordance with strict traditional rules of visual discretion, rules that are clearly set down in Malikite Law (one of the four schools of Moslem law). The owner is not allowed to build his house, or add to it in any way, without taking into account the morphology of the city. Above all, he must ensure that the height of his house does not enable him to look down into his neighbours' homes. He is also forbidden, as much by custom as by law, from walling off his terrace or installing windows or doors that overlook his neighbours' terraces or courtyards.

The traditional dwelling of the imperial cities is organized around an uncovered central courtyard surrounded by rooms and outbuildings. The layout varies according to the amount of land available, the way in which the living quarters have been organized and the social standing and tastes of the owner; the structure, however, remains the same. The walls surrounding the courtyard are often the only places on which ornamentation of any sophistication is displayed. The more prosperous the owner, the greater the wealth of polychrome *zillij*, stucco-work and mosaics. Leading off from the courtyard are two, three or four ground-floor rooms. On the sides of the courtyard where no living quarters have been built, the walls are either blind or fitted with a mural fountain or pavilion (*bartal*). The size of the courtyard and the manner in which it has been decorated are signs of social standing. From the middle-class home – comprised of one or more large patios, one side of which will sometimes give onto a garden – to the small house organized around a central room fitted with a latticed light-shaft, this private living-space can be designed and fitted out in any number of ways.

PATIO OF A "MIDDLE-CLASS" HOME, RABAT

This small patio is very tastefully designed:
a small garden, *zillij* paving,
carved arcades and porticoes.

BOU INANIA MADRASA, MEKNES

Institutions in which the Koran and Islamic science
and literature are taught, the *madrasas* of the imperial cities
are veritable masterpieces of architecture. The patios are surrounded
by richly carved porticoes and walls and paved with *zillij*.

The Art of Building in the Imperial Cities

The few examples of Idrissid architecture that have come down to us were influenced by the Arab capital of Kaïraouan in Tunisia and by the great oriental metropolis, Damas. The construction in Fez of the al Karaouyin and Andalous mosques in the middle of the ninth century marked the true beginnings of Islamic art in Morocco. From the middle of the tenth century, the country found itself at the crossroads of Ummayad Spain and Fatimid Ifriqiya. During the reign of the Almoravids, Moroccan art gradually freed itself from the influence of the Moslem West, giving birth to the Hispano-Mauresque style. The literature and art of Morocco were no longer inspired by Damas and Baghdad, while philosophic and scientific research, architectural and ornamental know-how now came from Cordoba and Granada. Contact with Andalusian civilisation turned the monarchs into builders. Fez and, in particular, Marrakesh became permanent centres of artistic creation where the artists of the empire put themselves at the service of the prince. The very forms of architecture employed were borrowed from Andalusia; henceforth, semi-circular horseshoe arches, calligraphy (often combined with floral motifs), stucco-work and stylised plant forms such as the acanthus leaf would form part of Morocco's ornamental heritage. The Almohads would turn that legacy to very good account, laying the foundations of an art that later dynasties could only imitate. The perfection of their minarets and city gates and the use of a rich decorative vocabulary marked a new advance in Hispano-Moroccan art.

The Merinids endeavoured to carry on the work of their predecessors. Lovers of art and literature, they welcomed poets, philosophers, jurists, scholars and artists from Andalusia and the Maghrib to their court. Influenced by the sophistication of the Andalusian courts, they adorned the cities of the kingdom with a whole host of monuments, and, in particular, with *madrasas*, Moslem colleges of which they were great builders. If Merinid art has neither the scale nor the forcefulness of Almohad art, it could vie with it in terms of harmony, elegance and beauty. The works carried out under the Saadian kings reflected an attachment to the glorious dynasties of the past, underwriting a tradition firmly established in Morocco by this stage. At the same time, their buildings are more monumental, graceful and free-floating and are marked by an abundance of decorative features.

SANCTUARY, MARRAKESH (DETAIL)

Above the two embrasures
are painted decorations and the
traditional roof of glazed green tiles,
green being the holy colour of Islam.

In both formal and spiritual terms, the works of the Alouite sovereigns, which include the many mosques of the imperial cities and the superb Al Cherratine *Madrasa* in Fez, perpetuate the skills and experience of the preceding centuries. At the same time, they express the splendour of a culture in its desire for renewal. The employment of new formulas in keeping with tradition and the substantial use made of materials such as *zillij* and painted wood give Alouite art an exuberance of sorts but a somewhat turgid style.

How were the four imperial cities constructed? Who built these lavishly decorated monuments that compel our admiration? In the history of Islamic architecture, we know more about the buildings and the patrons who commissioned them than we do about the artists who made them. We talk about Almoravid, Almohad and Merinid architecture, but almost never about the work of this or that architect or contractor. Construction was the collective achievement of a multitude of specialised trades (masons, joiners, plasterers, sculptors, carpenters, painters) and was overseen, not by an architect in the sense in which we understand that term today, but by a contractor. The plan of a building was drawn up orally and depended directly on professional skills acquired over the centuries. Complex buildings would sometimes be carried out over a long period extending beyond the lifetimes of the first generation of builders, and the initial shape of mosques or palaces would often be modified in the course of construction.

Shifts in architectural styles were determined by the tastes and habits of the country's masters and patrons. More often than not, palaces, mosques, *madrasas* and fortresses were the work of the prince, his family and the wealthy merchants who surrounded him. To erect a building, precious marble, granite and rare woods had to be brought in, sometimes from very far away, as well as craftsmen, each specialising in a particular branch of architecture or ornamentation. More value was attached to the decorative facings of walls and volumes than to the architecture as such. The inhabitants of the cities accorded little importance to the relationship of volumes and planes in space; what they admired more than anything was the abstract or epigraphic ornamentation, the sophistication of the mosaic work

DECORATIVE MOUKARNAS IN THE DAR AL MOQRI PALACE, FEZ
Moukarnas are stalactites delicately carved in plaster and sometimes decorated with paint work.

ORNAMENTAL WROUGHT IRON

Used to decorate the windows of the Bennani Palace in Meknes, ornamental wrought-iron takes the form of undulating arabesques and arcs.

DECORATIVE WOOD-WORK

Carved wood, sometimes painted, sometimes not, is very common in Moroccan ornamentation. Various designs are used : geometrical arabesques, vegetal motifs, even epigraphy.

SCULPTED STONE DECORATIONS

These delicate designs based on plant forms were made to ornament the mausoleum of Mohammed V in Rabat and are sculpted in soft stone.

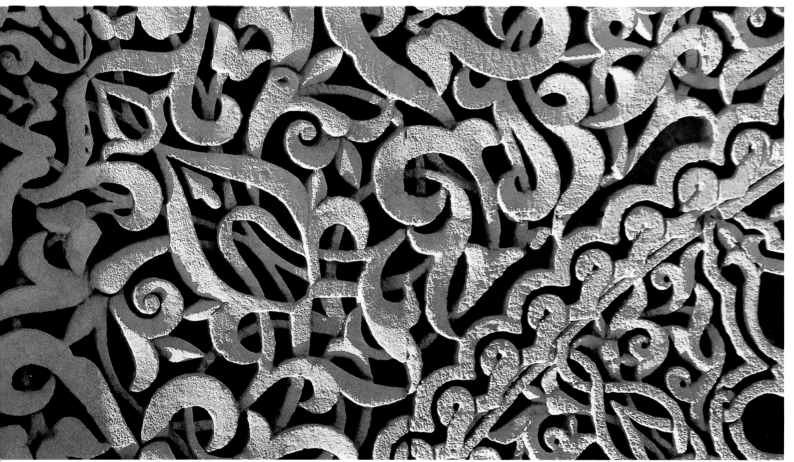

ZILLIJ-WORK

Used as decorative facings on the walls of civil and
religious buildings, these small pieces of brightly coloured glazed
clay vary in form and can be arranged in all kinds of geometrical
patterns based on the circle and the square.

ZILLIJ PAVING

Zillij are also used to pave floors,
though with greater sobriety than on walls.

and finely carved wood. Islamic architecture feeds on surprising contrasts
of this kind: the monochrome ornamentation of the outside walls contrasts
with the luminous splendour of its interiors, the arid outside spaces with
the unexpected splendours of the garden (*riyad*) within.

Arabo-Moslem ornamentation conforms to the strict religious norms of
Islam; the Hadith (a collection of actions, sayings and deeds of the
Prophet) is deeply hostile to the representation of living beings. This taboo,
based on the principle that it is impossible to imitate God's Creation, can
also be explained as a fear that false idols will continue to be worshipped
through the worship of icons. Skilled decorators rejected the imitation of
nature, devoting themselves exclusively to the representation of abstract
patterns. The technical skills and learning of these craftsmen, who were
accorded virtually the same status as scholars, enabled them to develop a
visual universe of ever-increasing complexity.

Moroccan aesthetics, enriched over the centuries by thousands of new
contributions, developed hand in hand with scholarly learning. Influenced
by the Greek, Persian and Hindu civilisations, rational and abstract
thought, astronomy, geometry and algebra filled the minds of Moslem
scholars. The works of Pythagoras (particularly the treatise on isometric
drawing), Vedic and magic squares (key elements in the underlying
matrices of Moslem ornamentation), polygons, algebraic curves used for
decorative plant forms, and spirals and calligraphic script are among the
borrowings from other civilisations developed by Moslem thinkers and
craftsmen. Affiliated to guilds, the latter were grouped together in brother-

hoods of initiates who would pass on to their fellow-members the interpretation of the hermetic codes to which they alone held the keys. By the sixteenth century, Moroccan decorative artists would make do with imitating their predecessors; the intellectual concepts which once governed the reproduction of forms were no longer the object of debate.

Complex geometrical compositions invite the eye to follow their development in a single, vigorous movement and, were they not obliged to break off at some point by the material constraints of the surface on which they appear, would continue on indefinitely in every direction. Within this system, that has neither beginning nor end, solids and hollows, inside and outside, echo one another. Locked in a state of perpetual contemplation, the gaze is never arrested by this or that central element, but follows a series of lines which cross continually back and forth, giving an almost tangible sense of infinity. The patterns and figures formed by mathematical combinations cover the entire object or wall in a never-ending series of repetitions.

PILLAR DECORATION
A recent piece of work directly inspired by the Hispano-Mauresque tradition. The lower area, inlaid with *zillij*, is prolonged by horizontal bands and a capital in sculpted plaster.

Amid the abundance of ornamental representations, three main groups can be made out: geometrical patterns, patterns based on curves (calligraphic script, floral decorations) and *moukarnas*, carved alveoli and stalactites (either corbelled or hanging). For facings, craftsmen had a wide range of materials at their disposal: glazed clay, plaster, marble, wood. The first of these was used for a form of inlaid facing known as *zillij*, in which polychrome faience tiles are arranged in elaborate patterns over walls, floors or ceilings, magnifying the architectural forms through the vibration of the colours. Hand-cut *zillij* of various shapes and colours are mounted on the wall in small geometrical patterns, forming motifs that are then repeated over the entire surface. The ornamental geometry of *zillij*-work is based on the straight line. Around the walls an epigraphic frieze of faience tiling will sometimes separate the lower surfaces, faced with *zillij*, from the upper areas, covered with chiselled plaster. This type of *zillij*-work consists of glazed clay tiles around the edges of which the craftsman will cut out decorative lettering and foliage. Finally, baked clay is used to manufacture the glazed green tiles (*qarmoud*) which cover roofs and porches. Characteristic of large buildings, these green tiles are used for mosques, wealthy homes and, in particular, palace buildings, and are a mark of distinction. The houses of wealthy city-dwellers are immediately recognisable from the outside on account of the green tiles covering their porches and oriel windows. These decorative compositions are not simply a clever combination of forms, they also display a remarkable sense of colour. Artisans would grind their own pigments from plants and minerals before applying them to their chosen medium. Their palette was dominated by different shades of blue, green and white, certain colours being used in particular for domes, minarets, terraces and walls. In all likelihood, craftsmen had their aesthetic preferences and accorded symbolic significance to their choices. The extensive use made in *zillij*-work of different gradations of blue, for example, gives the colour a special place in the history of Islamic architecture: originally associated with the cosmos, it is a window onto the Absolute.

The other colour with positive associations of which extensive use is made by craftsmen is green. According to the Koran, the colour, intimately bound up with nature and fecundity, is synonymous with abundance, creation and wealth. White, on the other hand, is essentially the colour of wisdom. For Moslem mystics like the Sufis, it is the sign of inner radiance, of the secret light and life-giving mystery of thought. In the Koran, white is associated with morality, honour and dignity, symbolised by the white winding-sheet in which the dead are shrouded.

ROOFS OF THE AL KARAOUYIN MOSQUE, FEZ

The roof of the mosque, like all religious buildings
in Hispano-Mauresque Moroccan architecture,
is covered with emerald-green varnished tiles.

1. Fez, the City of Letters

| Pages 26 - 27
GENERAL VIEW

From the olive-grove
south of the medina
can be seen the
minarets of the great
sanctuaries of Fez.

Fez, Morocco's oldest imperial city, is also the keeper of Hispano-Arabic history and tradition. Strategically placed at the intersection of two caravan routes stretching from the Mediterranean to Tafilalet and from the Atlantic to central Maghrib, the "Athens of Africa", as it is sometimes called (its university is older than the Sorbonne), acts like a magnet on the migrant populations that have enriched it with their cultures. Heir to a long history, it was chosen by several dynasties as the cultural and religious torch-bearer of the empire. At present the third-largest city in the country after Casablanca (the economic capital) and Rabat (the political capital), it remains one of the great centres of Islamic civilisation.

THE MEDINA

Seen from the hill
of the Merinid Cemetery,
the medina is girded round
with imposing crenellated
walls flanked by massive
watchtowers.

An Ancient Capital

Fez was founded by a descendant of the Prophet, Moulay Idriss (or Idriss the Elder), who later became the scourge of the Abbasid caliphs after taking part in an uprising in Mecca. In the course of his flight, Idriss stopped on the right bank of the Oued Fez, where in 789, before being poisoned by the vindictive caliphs, he established with the aid of small tribes of Berbers Morocco's first Islamic settlement, Madinat Fez. In 818, it provided refuge for thousands of Andalusian families driven out of Cordoba by the Umayyads, and the district where they lived was subsequently named after them, Adoua al Andalus. Idriss II then built a second town on the left bank, Al Alya (the upper town), which was soon filled with Arab families driven out of Kaïraouan, Tunisia some time around 824. This part of the town is now known as Al Karaouyin. The

BAB GUISSA

This gateway, which is still
in use but has lost its original
Almohad ornamentation,
links the medina
to the outside world.

two communities lived opposite one another and developed along different lines, but each contributed its own brand of urban culture and its own architectural skills and arts and crafts. Arabic became the dominant language, and the arts of pottery, wood-carving and sculpting in stucco flourished. The Islamic faith spread throughout the country and, in the same pious breath, the Al Karaouyin Mosque (857) and the Andalous Mosque were built.

Then followed a period during which Fez fell victim to the bloody rivalries and lust for wealth of the Umayyads of Spain and the Egyptian Fatimids. Wasn't this the lettered city that, in the early tenth century, was visited by scholars from Andalusia, come to consult the library of al Karaouyin? The gold in Guinea was also whetting appetites. The Idrissids finally gave way to the Almoravids, Saharan nomads who, though they founded their new capital in Marrakesh, did not neglect Fez. On entering the city in 1069, their sovereign, the "veiled Saharan" Youssef ben Tachfin, ordered the destruction of its walls. The two original towns now became one, with two bridges joining them. The Al Karaouyin Mosque became the economic and spiritual centre of the town, around which were assembled souks, *fondouks*, public baths, *norias* (waterwheels) and a distribution system for water. A fortress was built away from the medina, making Fez the military base of the new empire.

In 1145, Fez was conquered by the Almohads, whose empire extended from Tripoli to the Atlantic and from southern Spain to the Sahara; the town, after a period of destruction, enjoyed a period of unprecedented prosperity, and, by the thirteenth century numbered 120,000 houses. With its 700 mosques, its universities and Koranic schools, its scholars and officials, Fez was acknowledged by all to be Morocco's foremost economic and cultural metropolis. In 1212, the caliph al Nasser built a new fortress and ramparts, some of which still form part of the city walls.

In 1250, the Merinids succeeded in wresting the town from the Almohads. Being great builders, they made it the capital of the kingdom once again and set about adding to Fez el Bali – the old Fez made up of the two towns built by the Anadalusians and the Kaïrouans – a new town, Fez el Jedid ("the new"), built on a plateau and sufficiently vast to house the caliph, his attendants, his army and the court officials. This was El Medinat al Beyida, the "white town" in which the Merinids officially resided, the imposing walls of which enclosed a palace and a Great Mosque, to which would later be added two sanctuaries – the Al Hamra and Al Azhar mosques – the homes of the viziers and servants of the state, a market and, in the early fourteenth century, a Jewish quarter, the *mellah*. Fez was once again divided, with on one side the medina of city-dwellers, scholars, craftsmen, traders and labourers, and, on the other, the administrative and military city.

Unlike their predecessors, the Merinids had no ideological pretensions or plans for religious reform when they took over the country; the moment Morocco had been conquered, they sought to legitimise their seizing of the throne by defending Islam in Andalusia and encouraging

THE FTOUH CEMETERY
The Ftouh Cemetery is situated outside the rampart walls. In keeping with tradition, the gravestones are aligned in the direction of Mecca.

religious instruction. Their greatest achievement were the splendid *madrasas*, Koranic schools in which students could be housed and where a scholarship system was set up. The reputation of the mosque-university of al Karaouyin, where the most eminent scholars in western Islam taught courses in law, theology, grammar, logic and science, and of its library, rich in ancient manuscripts, date from this period.

The golden age of Fez lasted two centuries. The last years of the Merinid dynasty were marked by upheavals which, in 1471, brought the Wattasids to power. Fez entered on a long period of decline, further aggravated by the earthquake of 1522. When the Saadians seized control of the town in 1524 they moved their official residence to Marrakesh, and it wasn't until the coming of the Alouite (or Filali) dynasty that Fez would start to recover from the anarchy and fratricidal struggles that threatened to destroy the town. The first Alouite sultan, Moulay Rachid, chose Fez as the capital in 1666 and ordered the rebuilding of a city ravaged by more than a century of trials. At his bidding, the Kasbah al Khmis was built to the north of Fez el Jedid, bridges repaired and the *Madrasa* Al Cherratin ("the rope-makers' *madrasa*") built near the Al Karaouyin Mosque. His successor, the great Moulay Ismaïl (1646-1727), chose a new capital: Meknes. Fez went into a decline and the population started to thin out. Subject to the whims of short-lived princes and the ravages of warrior tribes (in particular, the Oudaia), Fez once more collapsed into anarchy. With the reign of Moulay Mohammed ben Abdellah, who restored order to the town and ushered in a period of peace and prosperity that would last right up to the beginning of the twentieth century, Fez was once again the capital, sharing the title with Marrakesh. King Hassan I (1873-1894) embarked on an ambitious series of building projects, including fortifications that took in both towns, a new palace next to Bab Boujeloud in the kasbah and a factory near Dar al Makhzen.

The establishing of the French Protectorate, on March 30, 1912 in Fez, brought about considerable changes. A modern city was built opposite the traditional medina, with new buildings, quarters for both rich and poor, an economic and commercial centre, an industrial zone and a hotch-potch of outlying allotments. It provided homes for part of the old imperial medina's professional classes, while a rural population that had been uprooted from its traditional environment and had no means to support itself moved into the downgraded older city.

From Fez el Bali to Fez el Jedid

Viewed from the hill on which the Merinid tombs are built, the medina of Fez resembles a tightly-knit mosaic punctuated with the occasional patio and indoor garden and hemmed round by powerful walls. Fortifications, towers and citadels are the more visible manifestations of the military architecture of what was once the capital of an empire. By the time of the Late Roman Empire, open cities were all but non-existent in Morocco; invasions from without and dynastic struggles from within had led the sovereigns to fortify the cities, and the capital in particular. Though the forms and techniques employed in Fez and throughout the rest of Morocco perpetuated the Roman and Byzantine tradition, they were upgraded to keep pace with the character of the attack and the degree of sophistication of the machinery of war.

Though rapidly overtaken by the development of offensive weapons in Europe in the form of artillery, fortified towns could still guarantee the supremacy of town over countryside and uphold order by containing the population within their ramparts. As in medieval European towns, fortifications made it possible not only to supervise the comings and goings of strangers and inhabitants, but also to levy taxes on goods. They also made it easier to separate three distinct social groups: the *makhzen* (the imperial administration), the inhabitants of the city and the foreign populations. Once outside the defensive walls, everything changed, including Moslem culture itself; beyond lay the "uncivilised" world of the countryside, vast tracts of unhallowed land.

The ramparts of Fez are anything but homogeneous in appearance, for they were built during different eras. Though no trace remains of the walls built under the Idrissid and Almoravid dynasties, the walls built in the twelfth century by the Almohad sovereign al Nasser were restored and further consolidated by the Merinids, while those of Fez el Jedid were built during the reign of the Merinid sultan Abou Youssef in 1269. The greater part of the ramparts consists of a single wall. Only Fez el Jedid is enclosed on the medina side by a double row of walls separated by a vast rampart walk designed to protect the royal city from assailants. The ramparts, which follow the curve of the hills to avoid having to build bulwarks, are roughly ten metres high. Crenellated throughout, they are punctuated with solid square towers, giving the them a massive and austere appearance. Four citadels (or *bordj*) inspired by Portuguese military architecture were added by the Saadians to make the town more secure: the first of these, the Tamdert Kasbah, is situated in the south-west of the town, near Bab al Ftouh, the other three being *bastioun* built by captive Christians. The corridor of walls linking Fez el Jedid to Fez el Bali is the work of the late-nineteenth-century sovereign, Moulay Hassan I.

The ramparts are pierced by monumental gateways – nine for the medina, six for the new city. The oldest of these, Bab Guissa and Bab al Mahrouq, situated in the north of the medina, were built in the Almohad era. Made with *pisé*, bricks or quarry stones, they are framed by two fortified, projecting towers forming a covered and sometimes stepped passageway. These vaulted, ill-lit corridors, reinforced by pilasters supporting horseshoe or ogival arches, were designed to slow up the enemy's progress during a siege. Being single-, double- and sometimes triple-stepped, they made it virtually impossible for cavalry to break

WALLS OF THE KASBAH OF THE CHRARDA

The citadel enclosed within these walls was built in 1670 by the first
Alouite sovereign, Moulay Rachid, and housed an Arab military tribe,
under the sultan's orders, responsible for defending the town.

FONDOUK

The ground floor serves as a stable for tradesmen's beasts of burden.

TRADITIONAL SHOP

Souk shops are rudimentary. These small, raised rooms are closed at night with wooden shutters.

POTTERY AND COPPERWARE

Pottery and copperware are among the specialities of a town renowned for its ancient tradition of crafts.

THE KISSARIYA

The market for precious goods (textiles, jewellery, perfume)
is covered with a wooden lattice to filter sunlight.

TRANSPORTATION MULEBACK

Mules are still the best way
of transporting things through
the narrow streets of the medina.

AL SEFARIN SOUK

Two apprentice coppersmiths
polish tea trays.

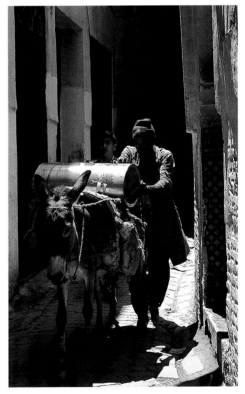

THE TANNERS' SOUK

Tanning is still carried out on the edge of town
near the Oued Fez in accordance with
time-honoured traditions. Before being delivered
to leather-workers, skins have to be softened up,
lubricated and smoothed by various means.
The actual tanning and dyeing of the leather
is done in vats.

through as a body. With the development of heavy artillery, the fortified walls of Fez became decorative constructions that contributed to the town's prestige and facilitated the levying of town dues. Up until the beginning of the twentieth century, they also helped protect the town from the bedouins, who possessed very little heavy artillery.

Decorated only on the outside, these gateways take the form of a bay, sometimes arched, as in Bab al Mahrouq, sometimes ogival, like the arch of Bab al Ftouh or the fourteenth-century gateway to the royal city of Bab Dekaken. The latter is surrounded with an ogival moulding of small, projecting, ornamental arcs, while the upper part is richly decorated with geometrical and calligraphic designs. On the spandrels inter-twining floral patterns can be found. The carefully bonded brick, which has since been replastered, enabled the builders to carve complex geometrical forms framing the bay of the door.

Passing under the monumental gateways to the medina – the largest in the Maghrib – the motley crowd presses on to the various souks. Making your way through a labyrinth lined with covered stalls and *fondouks*, the topography of which is unchanged since the twelfth century (the medina has been classified as part of world heritage by UNESCO), head for the *kissarriya*, the covered market for precious goods, where you will find perfumes, jewellery and silks to choose from, then on to the Al Karaouyin Mosque, the spiritual and economic centre of Fez and the mausoleum of the city's patron, Moulay Idriss. Alternatively, you can walk in the direction of al Nejjarin, the joiners' quarter, or of al Seffarin, where the coppersmiths work. In the Attarin Souk you will find sacks filled with spices, sugar-cones and bars of soap, while in the Ain Allou Souk you have leather goods and thousands of *babouches* (pointed slip-

HOUSES IN THE MELLAH

The Rue des Merinids in Fez Jedid is the old Jewish quarter. More well-to-do homes have balconies and windows decorated with carved wood and wrought iron.

THE AL NEJJARIN FONDOUK AND FOUNTAIN

Built in the mid-eighteenth century by Provost Adiyyel, this Alouite *fondouk* is the finest of its kind in Fez and a listed building.

pers) to choose from. If you are shopping for pottery, opt for the cobalt blues, the traditional colour of Fez. The bustling markets, where perfumes and colours compete for your attention, are a feast for the senses. Three main through roads lead out from the centre to the three main gates, Bab al Ftouh, Bab al Mahrouq and Bab Guissa. Professions are grouped together in *fondouks* or districts according to the goods or services they offer and organized hierarchically in relation to the centre. The *kisssariya* sells only luxury goods like jewellery, cords and braiding, perfume, textiles, candles and slippers. Cumbersome and less valuable objects, or those of particular interest to visitors from the countryside, are sold on the outskirts of town. At the Al Khmis Souk you will find the local coal market, while the tanneries, on account of the powerful stench they give off, are installed near springs or waterways. Around the Place des Seffarine can be heard the din of coppersmiths beating platters and

other recipients into shape. The cobblers are installed in small shops or *fondouks* near the market for *babouches*, while craftsmen who work directly with the outside world have set up shop around the gates of the city; this is notably the case with blacksmiths, whose stalls are situated at the Bab al Semmarin gate.

Some of the *fondouks* of Fez, such as Al Nejjarin (where the joiners store their wares) and Al Titwaniyin, run by Tetouans, have undeniable artistic interest. The former, which was probably built in the eighteenth century by an Alouite sovereign, is reached through a decorated gateway surmounted by a horse-shoe arch set into a facade notable for its size and for the delicacy of its ornamental designs. Al Nejjarin, a magnificent fountain inlaid with polychrome *zillij*, decorates the entranceway. The inner courtyard is surrounded by galleries adorned with balustrades and

DAR AL MAKHZEN GATE

The Dar Al Makhzen Gate is a recent construction
built by the master craftsmen of Fez el Bali
and scrupulously respects the traditions of the past.
The finely-chiselled bronze doors are furnished
with massive door-knockers, each decorated
with a five-pointed star, the symbol of Morocco.

moucharabieh, while the galleries themselves lead off into small rooms where wholesalers store their merchandise and retailers come for their supplies.

To the west of the old town can be found the imperial city of the Merinids. Girded round with powerful ramparts, it is made up of three distinct parts: in the centre, the palaces with their gardens and out-buildings; in the north, the working-class district, where the Christian militia used to live; and, in the south, the *mellah*, the first Jewish quarter in Morocco. The last of these was originally situated near the Jamaï Palace, before being moved close to the Royal Palace by the Merinid sovereign Abou Saïd, who had promised to protect its citizens against a new tax. Not that this stopped them from being subject to numerous constraints, such as being forbidden to wear *babouches* or mount their horses in town. These restrictions were lifted under the Protectorate. Running north-south from Bab Dekaken to Bab al Semmarin, a long artery cuts across the royal city, lined with the houses of dignitaries and servants of the *makhzen* and three mosques. Though its buildings were altered and restored under various dynasties, the main features of the original plan have been preserved. Dar al Makhzen, one of the current residences of the King and his family, is situated in the centre but is not open to visitors. This enormous, 200-acre estate conceals behind its walls a multitude of courtyards, pavilions, *mechouars* (esplanades where the royal army exercises and various open-air ceremonies are held), a menagerie, a mosque, a *madrasa* built in 1320 by the Merinid sultan Abou Saïd Othman and the spacious gardens of Lalla Mina. This huge complex also houses such old palaces as Dar Ayad al Kebira, built in the eighteenth century by Sidi Mohammed ben Abdellah, and Dar al Bahia, where official ceremonies are held. The monumental gates of chiselled copper which open into the palace from the Place des Alaouites are a recent addition built by the craftsmen of Fez. The architectural decorations are sumptuous throughout: sculpted plaster facings, carved and chiselled wood, polychrome *zillij* and hundreds of mosaic-covered columns and galleries stretching as far as the eye can see across vast patios adorned with marble fountains rival in beauty the huge, flowering gardens.

Palaces and Traditional Houses

Behind the scenes, not far from the shopping streets, is another Fez, peaceful, meditative and domestic, that seems to keep the eyes of strangers at bay. Made up of dark passages, unexpected barriers, blind alleys and bewildering twists and turns, the residential area is a group of sometimes closed enclaves and neighbourhood family groupings the organization and layout of which is known only to the Fassi. There is nothing conspicuous about the facades, no ostentatious display of wealth: only the high, blind walls with their ancient facings and, on occasion, the finely carved doors point to the social standing of the residents within.

DAR AL MAKHZEN GATEWAY (DETAILS)
The dominately blue *zillij* designs represent stylised flowers.

In this sacrosanct family environment, with its courtyards adorned with *zillij* under a rectangular blue sky and its bright, scent-filled Andalusian gardens, the indoor spaces are often masterpieces of architecture and ornamentation. Finely carved wood, sculpted plaster, stylish faience tiling and skilfully arranged fountains contrast with the austerity of the facade. Access to this residential zone is codified; no-one dares transgress its laws or shatter the meditative silence of its alleyways and houses. The ground-plan for normal houses and palaces in Fez never varies and is always composed of the same elements: an entrance-way, a courtyard and rooms and outbuildings. It is in the dimensions of the building, the quality of the materials employed and the complexity of the architectural ornamentation that differences are to be found. From the nineteenth century, certain aristocratic families had homes built on the other side of the ramparts, where it was possible to have a large garden.

The medina of Fez houses dozens of more or less secret palaces. One of these, the Dar Caïd bel Hassan, was built in the fourteenth century by a

Merinid citizen of some standing alongside the Bou Inania *Madrasa* and perfectly illustrates the architectural style of the period. This one-storied building, organized around a courtyard at the centre of which stand a small pond and a richly decorated wall-fountain, is a treasure-trove of carved wood, chiselled bronze, *zillij*, stucco-work and moucharabieh. Dar Demana, near Bab Guissa, is one of the palaces belonging to the family of Ouazanni sherifs and was built, again during the reign of the Merinids, by the vizier Demnati, who is said to have offered it to a member of this marabout family. This sumptuous palace dominates the steep incline known as Seqqaya Demnati. Enclosed within ochre-coloured walls, only its carved wooden doors enliven the monotony of its harsh façade. The living-quarters of this one-storied palace are organized around a strikingly elegant courtyard in which outbuildings, a stable and an Andalusian garden with a small pavilion can be found. Other middle-class homes dating back to the seventeenth and eighteenth centuries, such as Dar Sqalli, Dar al Alami, Dar Guennon and

DAR AL BATHA PALACE

Built by the sovereign Moulay al Hassan in the late nineteenth century, the Dar al Batha palace has a large Andalusian garden for royal receptions.

Dar 'Adiyel (the walls and porticoes of which are still decorated with stucco), conjure up the urban style and classical art of the well-to-do classes of the period. Dar al Batha is an unusual building which forms part of the palace complex of the imperial city. Situated in an old garden area watered by a *oued*, it was built at the end of the nineteenth century by King Moulay al Hassan I as a place in which to hold formal receptions. With its magnificent courtyard covered with faience tiling and decorated with a large ornamental pool and its enormous Andalusian garden paved round with polychrome *zillij* and featuring a white marble pedestal basin at its centre, al Batha, despite many later alterations, has retained its original plan. Today, it houses the Museum of Popular Arts and Traditions, with its collections of ancient pottery, eleventh-to-eighteenth-century astrolabes and Fez-stitch embroidering.

Dar al Moqri belongs to the noble family of the same name, one of whose ancestors was responsible for building royal palaces during the reign of Moulay al Hassan. His sons occupied important posts in the *makhzen* administration. Al Moqri Palace is arguably the most interest-

ing example of nineteenth- and early twentieth-century Moroccan architecture. Built in the Ziyat district on two-and-a-half acres of land where formerly there was nothing but orchards, it is made up of interconnecting buildings organized around patios paved with large, white marble flagstones separated by faience tiling and ornamented with star-shaped ponds. Delicate *zillij*-work covers the lower areas of the patio walls, while the ceilings of its many bedrooms are supported by elegantly carved beams. The galleries have blind arcades decorated with

open-work designs, and there is an Andalusian garden dotted about with music pavilions. In short, Dar al Moqri is an architectural splendour worthy of the *Thousand and One Nights.*

Mosques, Mausoleums and *Zaouiyas*

Each district of Fez contains one or more mosques. Among the profusion of places of worship, four different types can be distinguished: *jami*, the great mosques where the inhabitants of the city can celebrate Friday prayers; *masjid*, small mosques with minarets where Friday prayers can likewise be practised, provided a sufficient number of worshippers are present (some twenty-odd are needed in Morocco); *msid*, small oratories without minarets, used as places of prayer and for Koranic instruction; and *zaouiyas*, places of prayer in which the tomb of a saint can be found but which are also used for meetings of religious brotherhoods. All these places are closed to non-Moslems.

Fez is home to the most prestigious mosque in all Morocco, the Great Mosque of al Karaouyin. Founded in 857 by Fatima bint Mohammed al Fihri, a devout woman from Kaïraouan who spent her entire fortune building it, it is the seat of the traditional university and has been one of the principal intellectual centres of the Maghrib for more than a thousand years. Treated with respect by every dynasty down to the present day, the institution has been the object of careful restoration-work and development on the part of all the great city-building princes.

The original mosque was nothing more than a small oratory. Its ground-plan and architectural layout—a small courtyard with a *mihrab* indicating the direction of Mecca—are similar to those of all religious edifices built in the ninth century in the Maghrib. A hundred years after it was founded, in 956, alterations were made by the emir of the Zanata, who had a new minaret of quarry-stone built which can still be seen to this day. According to legend, the sword of Idriss II was found plunged into

AL KARAOUYIN MOSQUE

The door to the prayer-room is decorated with a stucco filigree highlighted by lines of blue paint. A overhanging roof of green glazed tiles further reinforces the somewhat imposing character of the entrance.

the tip of the minaret. It was only in 1135, during the reign of the Almoravid sovereign Ali ben Youssef, that the mosque acquired the dimensions it has today, being enlarged towards the south and considerably embellished. The works lasted fifteen years, during which time a magnificent *mihrab* was installed, the prayer-room was enlarged and to the right of the *mihrab* was placed a new pulpit or *minbar*, delicately carved with floral motifs. Handsome domes were placed over the newly built nave. The Saadians later removed from the courtyard two pavilions modelled on those in the Court of the Lions in the Alhambra Palace in Granada. As for the Alouites, they greatly enriched the liturgical fittings of the mosque.

What can a non-Moslem discover about the Al Karaouyin Mosque today? The interior is rectangular in shape and divided into two parts: a courtyard (*sahn*) and a prayer-room. The oblong courtyard, paved with polychrome *zillij*, is surrounded by bays leading into the pillared hall. At the centre, set over a square pond, is a basin carved from a single block of marble. To either side of the courtyard stand two pavilions with slender colonnettes and green-tiled, pyramid-shaped roofs (green being the

AL KARAOUYIN MOSQUE

A small oratory at the time it was built in the ninth century, the Al Karaouyin Mosque has since become one of the most celebrated sanctuaries in Morocco. The angle of the photo gives a good idea of the lay-out: a rectangular courtyard surrounded by a gallery and the green-tiled roofs of the nine naves of the prayer-room.

colour chosen by the Prophet to symbolise Islam). Each wall of the courtyard has a gallery supported by pillars crowned with semi-circular horseshoe arches. The mildness of the local climate means that the courtyard can be used as an open-air prayer-room. The numerous pillars supporting the ten naves and twenty bays break up the prayer-room into a multitude of identical volumes which appear to repeat themselves forever. The axial nave, with its cruciform pillars, is set off by a series of square, oblong or circular domes alternating with ribbed domes. The sheer profusion of decorative elements makes this place of prayer a haven of aesthetic contemplation.

Ever since the tenth century, this mosque-cum-university has also been famous for its library. The contents speak for themselves: 30,000 volumes, including ten thousand manuscripts and several famous incunabula, amongst which a ninth-century illuminated Koran, a manuscript by the philosopher Ibn Rochd (better known under the name of Averroes) and one of the original copies of the *Muqqadima*, the great summa of the fourteenth-century historian Ibn Khaldun.

From the outside the mosque easily goes unnoticed, since it does not stand out in any way against the overall pattern of the city. It no more towers above the unhallowed buildings than do the homes of men, and

AL KARAOUYIN MOSQUE

The pond and basin situated in the courtyard
are for performing one's ablutions.
Before prayers, the faithful must wash
their hands, mouth, face, ears, forearms
and feet three times.

its silhouette merges perfectly with the tightly-knit architecture of the medina. Reduced to a bare surface, and with no ostentatious decoration on show, its facade, with its smooth white surrounding walls, is conceived as an introverted space, like the city-dweller's home. Only the finely carved entrance door and the minaret show that it is a mosque.

In short, al Karaouyin is both Morocco's finest example of Hispano-Mauresque architecture and the most radiant illustration of its spiritual and intellectual influence.

Established on the opposite bank in the Andalusian quarter is the Andalous Mosque, built between 859 and 860, at the same time as al Karaouyin. According to legend, it was Fatima's sister, Mariam al Fihri, who financed the sacred building with the aid of a group of Andalusians. In 956, thanks to the generosity of the caliph of Cordoba, it was furnished with a minaret similar to that of its rival. In 1203, the Almohad sovereign Mohammed al Nasser made alterations to the oratory and the courtyard, giving them much the same form that they have today: a finely carved *mihrab*, a plain courtyard surrounded by a gallery and decorated at the centre with a marble pond. A fountain and a library were added later. Though the Merinids improved the appearance of the mosque, the Alouite monarchs did away with the ornamentation of

AL KARAOUYIN MOSQUE

The prayer-room is broken down into naves and bays. The decoration is very strict, ground and pillars being simply covered with matting; only the *mihrab*, towards which the faithful turn in prayer, is the object of more elaborate ornamentation.

their predecessors in the course of restoration work. This plain building covered with twin-sloping roofs still preserves a domed minaret from the Zanata period, however, along with a monumental door crowned by an exceptionally beautiful carved cedar-wood porch.

Another sanctuary that stands out at a distance is the El Rsif ("the paved street") Mosque. Situated next to the souks, it was built during the reign of Moulay Mohammed ben Abdellah (1757-1790), half-way up the cliff overlooking the river. Its elegant minaret, decorated with green faience tiles, confers a certain majesty on the building, though it is no higher than that of al Karaouyin; the latter originally towered above all the other minarets in the city so that, each Friday, the black flag that was hoisted there to indicate the time for prayer would be visible to all.

Other sanctuaries merit special attention: the Al Chrabliyin Mosque (named after the slipper makers), built in the Merinid period, with its fine polychrome minaret; the Bab Guissa Mosque; and the Abou al Hassan Mosque, founded in 1341 by the Merinid sultan of the same name, with its imposing entranceway.

Fez el Jedid, the royal city, likewise takes pride in its very ancient mosques, most of which date from the Merinid period. Let us mention the most important of these, beginning with the Great Mosque, Jamaa al Kebir. Founded in 1279, it is surmounted by a charming minaret made of brick and decorated with ornamental carvings and polychrome faience tiles. Little remains of its former decorations, for it was restored and extended under various reigns. In its overall appearance, however, it is a perfect reflection of that Merinid art which, while preserving the forcefulness of Almohad architecture, already possessed the decorative profusion and delicacy of sixteenth-century art. It was in this sanctuary that the great Merinid sovereign, Abou Inan, was probably buried, and sultans have been coming here to pray for centuries. Mention should also be made of the Al Hamra ("the red") Mosque and of the small Jamaa el Azhar Mosque built by Abou Inan, with the unaffected beauty of its minaret, its elegantly carved portal (thought to have been imported from Andalusia) and the delicate stucco-work of its oratory.

You need to return to Fez el Bali to find the most revered sanctuary in the whole of Morocco, the *zaouiya* of Moulay Idriss, the second sovereign of the Idrissid dynasty. Built in the spiritual and economic centre of Fez, the sanctuary is an average-sized building. All the streets leading to it are closed off half-way along by wooden beams marking the limits of the *horm*, the holy place par excellence, and barring the way to beasts of burden. Once inside the mosque, no Moslem could be arrested, for he enjoyed a right of asylum there. After a period of neglect that lasted several centuries, the *zaouiya* was restored in 1437 under the Merinids.

GATEWAY OF THE AL TIJANI ZAOUIYA

Sidi Ahmed al Tijani was a Sufi born in Algeria who was persecuted by the Turks and took refuge in Fez. The brotherhood he founded spread mostly through black Africa, and it was largely with pilgrims from those countries in mind that this place of prayer was built.

As for the cult of Moulay Idriss, after falling into abeyance, it was taken up by the Wattasids (1472-1554), who revived the ceremonies practised around his tomb. The Saadians enlarged the mausoleum, and, between 1717 and 1719, at the prompting of Moulay Ismaïl, the inhabitants completely redesigned the building, conferring on it its current wealth of ornamentation. An enormous domed hall encloses the tomb of the saint, which is covered with a carved wooden canopy inlaid with copper and gold. For centuries, the sanctuary has attracted not only the inhabitants of Fez, who deeply revere the patron saint of the city, but also the inhabitants of other regions of Morocco in search of *baraka* ("good fortune"). They come to touch the saint's tomb through a small open-work copper plate placed in the side. The tomb has become a place of pilgrimage, accompanied by a precise ritual. Once a year, on the feast of the Mulid (the anniversary of the Prophet's birth), all the trade associations lead off in a procession from the tomb in a state of religious fervour enlivened by chanting and music. Previous to this, offerings and sacrifices have been duly made to Moulay Idriss in exchange for his protection and blessing.

Other much-frequented *zaouiyas*, such as Sidi Ahmed al Tijani, Sidi Abdelkader al Fassi and Sidi Ahmed al Chaoui, are also important landmarks of the town.

But Fez, which possesses dozens of sanctuaries and places of prayer and religious instruction, also has a different category of religious building designed for teaching: the celebrated *madrasas*.

Merinid *Madrasas*

The Merinid sovereigns were the greatest builders of *madrasas* in the Moslem West. In founding these holy centres, they hoped to win the loyalty of the *ulama* (doctors of law) and pass themselves off as the great patrons of Islam. There was also another motive for their religious zeal: Morocco at the time was prey to a religious and mystical fervour that was somewhat heterodox and irreverent; only a return to Moslem orthodoxy could nip the heresy in the bud. For this reason, thousands of young city-dwellers and country folk were given the benefit of free religious education in its purest Sunni form, in keeping with Malikite tradition.

Most of the *madrasas* were built between 1300 and 1350. The medieval student entered by a minutely carved door – the building's only distinguishing feature, for the outside walls are blind – and found himself in a courtyard decorated with *zillij*, often equipped with a pond and fountain for performing one's ablutions. The courtyard would be surrounded with the most richly ornamented walls and porticoes in the entire city. Illustrative of the refinement of Hispano-Mauresque architecture, they constituted the latter's coat-of-arms, as it were. On the ground floor, a large hall (the *harem*) is used for study and prayer, while on the upper floor are small, bare cells where the students sleep. Some *madrasas* even have a minaret, a feature they have in common with mosques.

ZAOUIYA OF MOULAY IDRISS

Behind this magnificently carved door
lies the tomb of Idriss II, the founder
and patron of the city of Fez.

BOU INANIA MADRASA

Merinid *madrasas* were built
in the fourteenth century and ornamented
with a particularly harmonious
combination of wood and stucco.

AL SAHRIJ MADRASA

The pool in the inner courtyard creates an atmosphere
conducive to meditation and study. The side galleries
are closed off with moucharabieh panels.
The delicate lattice-work, made of an assemblage
of turned wood, allows you to see without being seen.

BOU INANIA MADRASA

From the outside only their finely carved doors distinguish *madrasas* from other buildings. The geometrical device employed here, known as a "Solomon's seal", consists of an eight-pointed star made with two superimposed squares.

BOU INANIA MADRASA

Designed as a place for study and worship, the *madrasa*
is finely carved throughout, as can be seen from its minaret.

AL ATTARIN MADRASA

With its harmonious proportions and
sophisticated ornamentation, the Al Attarin
Madrasa is one of the finest Merinid buildings.

Situated near the Al Karaouyin Mosque and the Al Attarin Souk, the *madrasa* of the al Attarin ("the spice merchants") is among the most attractive in Morocco. Built between 1323 and 1325 by the sultan Abou Saïd Othman, it has all the basic elements that make up these colleges: a prettily decorated entranceway; a courtyard paved with brown and white *zillij* with a fountain for ablutions and four facades lined, along the bottom, with the same polychrome faience tiling used to decorate the pillars; and, finally, a prayer-room with a *mihrab* opening onto the courtyard through a door with a pelmet arch delicately ornamented with chiselled plaster lambrequins and alveoli. The students' rooms, situated on the first floor, open onto the patio via balustered windows of carved wood. The Al Attarin *Madrasa* is held to be, after that of Bou Inania, the greatest masterpiece of the Hispano-Mauresque architecture of the Merinid builders.

The Al Sahrij *Madrasa* ("of the pond") is linked to an architectural complex made up of two *madrasas* built in 1321, during the reign of Abou al Hassan: al Sahrij and al Sebbayin ("of the seven"), so named because the seven ways of reading the Koran were taught there. Beautifully decorated with intricate designs of *zillij*, sculpted plaster and carved wood,

Pages 64-65
AL ATTARIN MADRASA

Once the plaster applied to the walls had been carefully smoothed
the designs were added with the aid of a stencil. The areas cut
out in this way gave sculptors the exact shape of the composition.

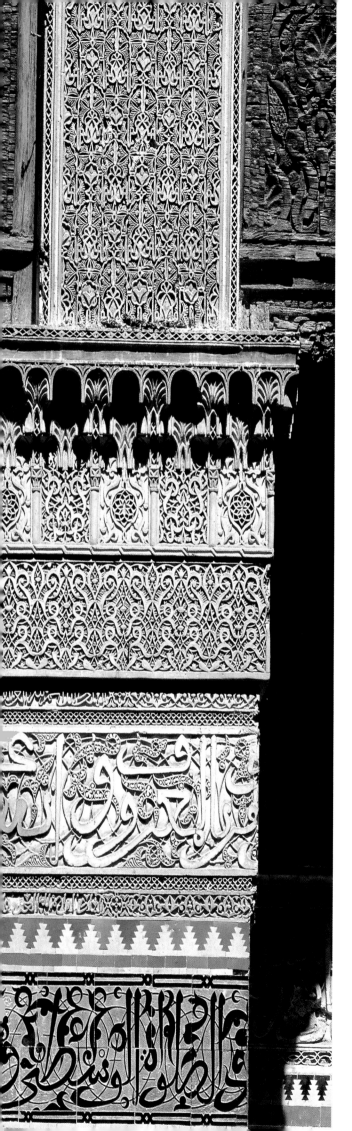

this double *madrasa* presents a sumptuous cross-section of Andalusian ornamentation in the Merinid period.

Finally, Bou Inania is the most monumental and prestigious *madrasa* ever built by the Merinids and the only religious building in Morocco open to non-Moslems. Built by the great sovereign Abou Inan between 1350 and 1355 in the business district far from al Karaouyin, and planned as a cathedral mosque destined for Friday prayers and religious in-struction, this *madrasa*, in keeping with the wishes of its founder, is the only one in Morocco endowed with both a university chair and a minaret. The sovereign, moreover, specified the uses to which the building was to be put on a marble slab attached to the eastern wall of the prayer-room, in which he takes upon himself the title of *amir al muminin* ("commander of the faithful").

It is the many and varied functions of the building that are responsible for its complexity. Bou Inania has a symmetrical plan. Rectangular in shape, this one-storied building surrounds a square, uncovered court-yard paved with marble and bordered on three sides by a cloister, the pillars of which are linked by delicately carved wooden panels. Facing the main door is the prayer-room with its *mihrab*. On the ground and first floors can be found the usual small cells for students. Two square teaching rooms form niches to either side of the patio, in the manner of a Persian alcove. A handsome minaret rises up at right angles to the building. The decoration, which is extremely abundant, combines exuber-ance and harmony, with Andalusian-style faience tiling, stalactite-like stucco-work known as *moukarnas* around the windows, steps of onyx and finely carved bronze doors. Everywhere, the black calligraphy of Kufic script projects its arabesques into the spaces defined by cedar-wood moucharabieh. The facade of the prayer-room is beautifully carved. With perfect symmetry, it opens out from a central door with a pelmet arch itself surmounted by a flat arch and three open-work partitions. To either side of the door, cavities in the form of carved niches add a finishing touch to the ornamental profusion of the wall, composing a masterpiece of harmony that is a tribute to the skill of Merinid craftsmanship but, above all, an illustration of the firm determination of a builder-king who dared to proclaim himself caliph. These marvellous monuments were all built at the prompting of princes to underwrite their glory and fix themselves in people's minds. Fez, the most radiant of the imperial cities, has profited from its dual status as a city of the *mahkzen* and a religious and cultural centre to enrich its heritage. Even when a dynasty deserted it, it remained a royal city, as the nobility of its stones still testifies to this day.

AL ATTARIN MADRASA

The pillars supporting the gallery are made by superimposing different horizontal bands: calligraphy (cut out in the *zillij* or sculpted in plaster), friezes decorated with arabesques, and *moukarnas*.

2. Marrakesh, the City of the Seven Saints

PALM GROVE

The Almohads used a sophisticated network
of underground canalisation, the *khettaras*,
to irrigate vast tracts of greenery
in an otherwise arid region. According
to legend, the palm grove grew from
date-seeds spat out by the soldiers
of Youssef ben Tachfin.

Pages 68 - 69

RAMPARTS

Dominated by the snow-capped peaks
of the High Atlas mountains, the Almohad
ramparts of Marrakesh have lost none
of their original allure. Eight metres high
in places, these ochre-coloured walls extend
nineteen kilometres around the city.

The capital of an empire the moment it was founded, Marrakesh, Morocco's southern metropolis, has always had an aura of prestige for having given its name to the entire kingdom. Yet, for all its fame, the city has never been classed as a *hadariya* city (or urban centre of civilisation) by historians of Morocco. Though once home to a large colony of Andalusians, it stands out on account of the unusual character of its inhabitants, who are very different from the middle-class city-dwellers of Fez or Rabat. Built in an oasis in the middle of the Haouz plain at the foot of the Atlas mountains, Marrakesh has always been the city of the Berbers and the nomadic desert tribes. It is, moreover, in the practice of Sufism and the cult of the saints dear to those peoples that the city has its roots and traditions. It is here, above all, that the seven great saints or *wali* laid to rest in the mausoleum of the medina are worshipped. The most popular of these, Sidi bel Abbès, is also the city's patron.

The Berber Metropolis

Marrakesh is in large part the work of two Berber dynasties: the Almoravids of the Sahara and the Almohads of the High Atlas mountains. Abou Bakr, the great Almoravid emir, is said to have been the first to build, in 1062, a kasbah of stone north of what is today the Koutoubiya. This was rapidly turned into a citadel by his cousin and

THE AGDAL

Planted with palm trees, olive trees
and fruit trees, the royal gardens are
three kilometres long and watered
by a gigantic reservoir dating
from the twelfth century.

successor, Youssef ben Tachfin, who, in the space of a few years, founded an empire stretching from the Atlantic to Algiers and from Spain to the Sahara. Marrakesh profited from these conquests and from the riches (notably gold and ivory) brought back by the caravans. When Youssef died at the age of a hundred, his son, Ali ben Youssef, gave the city an appearance worthy of that empire. Craftsmen and architects were brought in from Andalusia, and all manner of artists, philosophers and writers flocked to his court. Mosques, palaces, *hammams* and ramparts were built, for the greater glory of the Hispano-Mauresque style. Marrakesh was endowed with an enormous royal palace, of which only a few vestiges are left today, as well as a sumptuous mosque, of which only the ornamented dome *(Koubba)*, Al Baroudiyin, remains. Ali ben Youssef was also responsible for constructing the *khettaras*, a complex system of underground canalisation that harnesses the ground waters of the Atlas to irrigate the great plain of Haouz, keeping the palm grove flourishing and supplying the inhabitants of the town with water. This remarkable feat of civil engineering, which transformed Marrakesh into an orchard, is still used to this day. In the meantime, the Almoravids, whose life-style and culture kept them aloof from religious dogma, were under threat from raids by the Almohads, strictly orthodox Moslems united under the leadership of the preacher Ibn Toumert.

Coming down from the mountains, the Berbers laid siege to Marrakesh, which Ali had been protecting with powerful walls ever since 1126. The fortifications, however, proved insufficient, and in 1147 the town fell into the hands of the Almohad sultan Abd al Moumen. Urged on by reformist *ulama*, he ordered all palaces and mosques "marked by sinfulness" to be demolished. Only the Al Baroudiyin dome (*Koubba)* and parts of the city ramparts escaped his purifying zeal. The conqueror of this vast empire took the title of caliph, like the masters of Baghdad and Cordoba. Marrakesh became the centre of western Islam and, protected by the Berbers of the High Atlas, for three quarters of a century enjoyed a period of peace that was favourable to the development of trade.

The Almohad sovereigns, as it turned out, were also builders. At the very beginning of his reign, Abd al Moumen began work on a masterpiece of Hispano-Mauresque architecture that was to leave its mark on countless subsequent constructions: the Koutoubiya Mosque, built on the site of the Almoravid Palace. A generation later, the old Almoravid citadel being too small to house the entire court, Abou Yakoub Youssef (1163-1184) added to the town a new district sheltered by ramparts, the kasbah, and laid out the garden of the Agdal. His son, Yakoub al Mansour (1184-1199), a tireless builder, then added a new imperial town to the south, consisting of twelve palaces, a mosque, a hospital and a garden (the Merinid capital, Fez el Jedid, is an exact replica of this). All that remains are the mosque and the beautiful palace gates, now known as Bab Agnaou. The Almohads were thus responsible for introducing in Marrakesh the large gardens (*agdal*) and large ponds (*sahrij*) that delighted and inspired so many scholars of the Middle Ages. In contrast with the lavishly decorated Almoravid and Andalusian buildings, Almohad constructions display a perfect conceptual and artistic unity characterised by elegant lines, simple forms and an austere aesthetic in keeping with the religious puritanism of that dynasty. Architecture was not the only legacy Marrakesh received from the Almohads. Economic relations founded on the trading of leather, sugar and ceramics also flourished with Spain, as did intellectual exchanges. It was in Marrakesh that the famous philosopher Averroes (Ibn Rochd) wrote certain of his commentaries on Aristotle.

The death of Yakoub al Mansour marked the decline of the Almohad dynasty. In 1212, the sovereign's son was crushed by the Christians at the famous battle of Las Navas de Tolosa, which sounded the beginning of the retreat of Islam in Andalusia. A long period of anarchy, fratricidal struggles, famine and epidemics undermined the Almohad government, which finally collapsed in 1276. Marrakesh had already been conquered in 1269 by a new dynasty, the Merinids. Since the latter had their residence in Fez, Marrakesh ceased to be the capital for two centuries, being

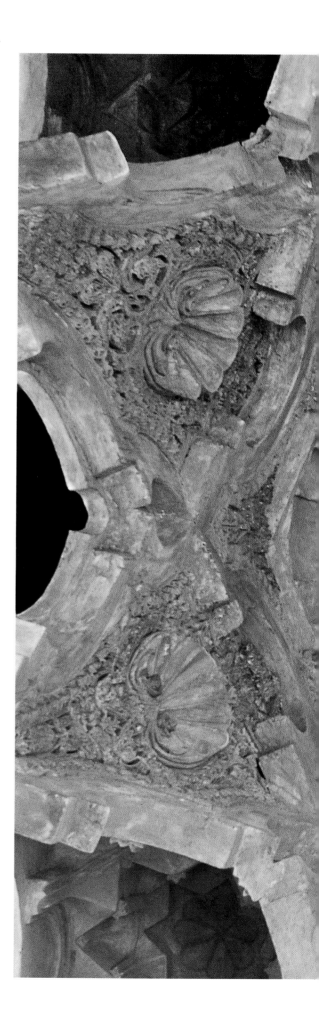

AL BAROUDIYN KOUBBA

The Al Baroudiyn cupola was built in the early twelfth century by the Almoravids. Its exuberant, Andalusian-style ornamentation is one of the few works of artistic interest to have been spared from destruction by the Almohad purists.

MAUSOLEUM

The worship of saints in Marrakesh has its roots in the religious fervour of the fifteenth century and is still thriving to this day. Mausoleums were built wherever a saint had passed, and in some cases contain their tombs.

relegated to the role of southern metropolis responsible for the African gold routes. It was this city in ruins, depopulated by famine, that, in 1522, was entered by the Saadians, whose name would come to symbolise the rebirth of Morocco. One of their chiefs, Ahmed al Mansour (also known as al Dehbi, "the golden one"), spurred on by victory at the Battle of the Three Kings (1578) and the conquest of Tombouctou (1591), used funds from the Portuguese war reparations and the gold that had been recovered – three tons are said to have been brought back from the expedition – to enhance the city he had chosen as his residence. To the north of the kasbah he built a huge official palace, al Badi ("the Incomparable"), inspired by the Alhambra, whose Court of the Lions it copied. Since Marrakesh had taken in, after the storming of Granada by the Catholic kings in 1492, the last Moslems to be expelled from Spain, the Mudejars, an Andalusian influence can be seen in the edifices built from the sixteenth century on. Carrara marble at the time is said to have cost the same price as sugar. What is certain is that the wealth of Marrakesh was based on morocco leather, the profits from which went into rebuilding the town. By the end of the sixteenth century, the *mellah*, or Jewish quarter, housed the largest Jewish community in Morocco.

Several years after the death of Ahmed al Mansour, Morocco underwent a deep crisis, in part brought about by marabout agitation, in part by the debility of the last sovereigns and their domestic squabbles. In 1668, Marrakesh succumbed to the Alouites. Under their reign, the capital of

MAUSOLEUM
Usually situated outside the rampart walls,
these small buildings have no architectural
pretension but are nevertheless
crucial religious landmarks
for the cities' inhabitants.

the kingdom was transferred first to Fez, then to Meknes. Every so often, however, a handful of sultans would elect Marrakesh the capital, marking their passage by important building works. The first sovereign of the new dynasty, Moulay Rachid, had his residence in Marrakesh until the time of his accidental death in the gardens of the Agdal. His successor, Moulay Ismaïl, took no interest in the city, pulling down the palaces of the kasbah in order to use their materials in Meknes, his new imperial capital. Fortunately, the sultan Moulay Mohammed ben Abdellah, who had a soft spot for the city of which he once been governor, made it his capital. From 1757 to 1790, his reign over a country that had now been pacified and was in the midst of reconstruction profited the city greatly. The moment he came to power, the sultan launched an ambitious restoration programme for the kasbah and the ramparts, laid out several gardens and built a new royal palace with outbuildings and gardens, as well as the official Great Mosque, the Berrima palace and the mosques in the al Badi and Chtouka neighbourhoods. After the death of Moulay Mohammed ben Abdellah, Marrakesh went through a long period of poverty and unrest. Throughout the nineteenth century, the city echoed to the sounds of fratricidal struggles and palace revolutions that the European powers turned to their advantage. In 1912, under the Protectorate, the resident general, Louis Hubert Lyautey, invited the town-planner Henri Prost to modernise the city. The latter created a new district, the Gueliz, next to the medina to house the administration of the Protectorate.

Marrakesh the Red

Any traveller flying in to Marrakesh today will have noticed the pattern of the capital as he comes in to land. The old city, enclosed within ramparts, stands out with its buff-coloured ochres. Offset by enormous, dark green gardens watered day in, day out, by irrigation channels that are centuries old, this warm colour serves as a backdrop to ponds reflecting the silvery mass of olive trees and the majestic palm trees of the Almoravids. This dazzling greenery, in striking contrast with the wide, arid plains of the Haouz stretching all the way to the snow-covered peaks of the Atlas mountains, makes Marrakesh an oasis of calm and gives it a somewhat fairy-tale air. Rising up out of the desert, this southern city, for all the work done by the builders from the north, still has the soul of its nomadic founders. Dominated for more than eight centuries by the elegant minaret of the Koutoubiya, the elder sister of the Giralda of Seville, Marrakesh has the majesty and grace of an Andalusian city. Marrakesh is surrounded by imposing walls some ten kilometres in length, six to eight metres high and one-and-a-half to two meters deep, made from clay and lime. Their irregular outline, unchanged since the Almoravid period, gives the city a distinctively medieval feeling. They are reinforced by powerful watchtowers and pierced by six monumental gateways in the Hispano-Mauresque style, a number of which have retained their original shape and stepped passageways. One of the most remarkable of these is the gateway to the kasbah, Bab Agnaou (from the Berber for "speechless black ram"), formerly the main entrance to the Almohad Palace. It has lost the two towers that used to frame it. Are we to believe the legend according to which the stones with which it was built were brought from Anadalusia by Moors driven out of Spain? A decorative frieze of red and turquoise sandstone carved with verses from the Koran serves as a framework for four interlocking semicircular arches, each with its own ornamental designs. This was the arch under which Yakoub al Mansour passed when entering his palace, perhaps glancing up at the heads of executed criminals on display there. The other gateways also have stories to tell. Bab Doukkala, in the north-west wall, derives its name from the Doukkala region, where the leper quarter used to be established. Bab al Khemis ("Thursday's gate"), so called because a cattle market is held there on that day, opens onto the road to Fez, and its panels are said to have been brought back from Andalusia by an Almoravid prince. Bab Debbagh, with its five-angled defence mechanism still intact, leads into the tanners' quarter, which is situated outside the medina near the Oued Issil on account of the noxious odours given off by that activity. Bab Hmar ("the red gate") is an Alouite legacy and gives access to the *mechouar* adjoining Dar al Makhzen when the king is not in residence in Marrakesh. Opposite the ramparts are cemeteries

BAB AGNAOU GATEWAY

In the twelfth century, the Bab Agnaou gateway was the entrance to the Almohad sultan's palace. The sober composition surrounding the bay is characteristic of gateways built during that dynasty.

and small, domed mausoleums dedicated to venerated marabouts charged with protecting the city from disaster.

Inside the ramparts, small, low houses built in *pisé* alternate with luxurious homes built by court officials and wealthy merchants. The buildings, however, do not extend over the entire area (which is immense) contained within the walls. Vast gaps in the city's eastern, western and, above all, southern flanks accommodate magnificent gardens, such as the famous Agdal, planted in the twelfth century by the Almoravids with fig, apricot, orange and olive trees and several times enlarged. The ruins of a Saadian palace are reflected in its Almohad ponds, and a green-tiled pavilion is concealed among the garden paths. Like other Moroccan cities, Marrakesh is made up of three parts: the medina proper, the kasbah and the *mellah*. Each was originally independent of the others and closed its rampart gates at night, making it very difficult to move about town. The area that unites them is the great Place Jamaa al Fna, a gigantic street-theatre square of musicians, *gnaoua* dancers, storytellers, snake-charmers, monkey-leaders, clairvoyants, witches and apothecaries that attracts both local inhabitants and visitors from the countryside and abroad. In the morning it is used as a market for fruit, vegetables and spices and for a variety of second-hand goods (medicines, dentures and spare parts of every conceivable description); in the evening it is given over to cheap, open-air restaurants. Dominated by the masterly minaret of the Koutoubiya, this huge square is the very heart of Marrakesh, the place where its streets converge and where the inhabitants of the city rub shoulders with foreigners. Though no building of any particular note is to be found there, the square is a repository of

THE MEDINA

The warm-coloured streets of the medina are broken up by arcades, dark areas and sudden shafts of light. Behind its anonymous walls – some plastered, some painted – sumptuous palaces are sometimes concealed.

ancient folk traditions classified by UNESCO a part of the oral heritage of mankind.

Starting from Jamaa al Fna, a dense network of narrow streets spreads throughout the city like a spider's web. Its design is simpler and more coherent than that of Fez. The main roads that run through the city link the rampart gates and the business quarter. The enormous souks of Marrakesh begin at Jamaa al Fna and, as in all the imperial cities, are organised in the north and east according to profession. At the centre is the *kissariya*, the market for precious goods, while all around is an inextricable cat's cradle of streets protected from the sun by wooden latttice-work.

Not far from the Qassabin Souk (for spices and dried fruits) is the Smarin Souk for fabrics. This is followed by the Al Ghazal Souk or wool market. Next come the Al Zrabia Souk, where Berber auctioneers sell rugs in the late afternoon, the Al Kebir Souk (for leather goods), the Place Rahba al Qdima (formerly the slave-market but today lined with apothecaries'shops), the Souk of the Chouari (where lemon- and walnut-wood is carved), the Smata Souk (for *babouches*), the al Fagharin Souk for blacksmiths, and the dyers'and coppersmiths'souks. Unlike Fez, Marrakesh has never had much of an export industry and serves, above all, as an enormous market for the region. Only the leather industry, which occupies a very large area in the network of souks, produces manufactured goods that are exported as far away as Egypt and western Africa. Finally, only a few of the *fondouks* are used to stock wholesale merchandise, since most of them are used at night to accommodate the city's foreign population.

LIPSTICK
Lipstick is made with poppy-dye.

WATER SELLER

With a leather water-skin on his back
and a goblet in his hand, the *guerrab* is one
of the more picturesque figures of the medina;
offering refreshment to the stroller.

PLACE JAMAA AL FNA

This colourful square can't be ignored
and in the morning houses a large market overflowing
with local produce (spices, herbs, amber, fruit, handicrafts).
In the afternoon it becomes a street-theatre packed
with musicians, dancers and story-tellers
that continues late into the night.

IN THE SOUKS

The souks start at the Place Jamaa al Fna and are arranged
by profession, as is the custom. Dyers hang their fabrics from
the latticed roofs, a cobbler displays some *babouches* he
is repairing and a wood-worker makes handles for meat skewers.

THE FEAST OF THE THRONE

Every year on March 3,
Moroccan notables assemble
in front of the Royal Palace
to renew their allegiance to
the king.

Next to the medina is the kasbah, the royal city of Marrakesh. Close and at the same time distant from one another, these two units are more united than divided, unlike those in Fez. The architecture of the kasbah gives it a temperate, human, welcoming air; this princely city is not a symbol of the will to power of its sovereigns. Though separated by a wall, the prince and his entourage did not try to protect themselves from the people, unlike in Meknes, where triple ramparts and esplanades formed an insurmountable barrier. The walls of the kasbah bespeak a certain confidence between the Almohad sovereigns, the inhabitants of the city and the rural population. The imperial city has preserved the structure handed down to it by that great dynasty, which consists of three parts: one public and utilitarian, made up of large reception areas such as the *mechouar*; one private, reserved for the harem and those close to the sovereign; and a third made up of gardens, huge orchards and two enormous ponds. By turns devastated, restored or entirely reconstructed under successive dynasties, these different structures are still used to this day. The Almohad Kasbah having proved too spacious for the Saadians and the Alouites, townsfolk moved into the royal city, building modest living-quarters amid the former homes of court dignitaries and the lodgings of the militia and the imperial guard.

Small mosques were built to satisfy the needs of a growing population. Today, the wall separating the two towns has all but vanished; with the exception of the palace, the districts of the kasbah are all but indistinguishable from the medina. As for the *mellah*, built under the Saadians, it has shed its initial population and become a district much like any other.

From the Koutoubiya to "the Mosque of the Golden Apples"

Inaugurated in 1158 by Abd al Moumen, who, after pulling down all the Almoravid constructions, wanted to consecrate his seizing of power in Marrakesh by building new sanctuaries, the mosque of the Koutoubiya owes its name to the hundred *koutoubiyin*, or booksellers, who occupied the forecourt. Being wrongly oriented in relation to Mecca, it was replaced almost immediately by a second building that was completed by Abd al Moumen's successor, Abou Yakoub, in 1199. Shaped like a trapezium, the new Koutoubiya was 90 metres wide and 58 metres deep and was one of the largest mosques in the Moslem West. Made to hold 20,000 worshippers, it is composed of sixteen parallel naves of equal width set at right angles to the *qibla* (the wall indicating the direction of Mecca) and a median nave that is wider than the rest.

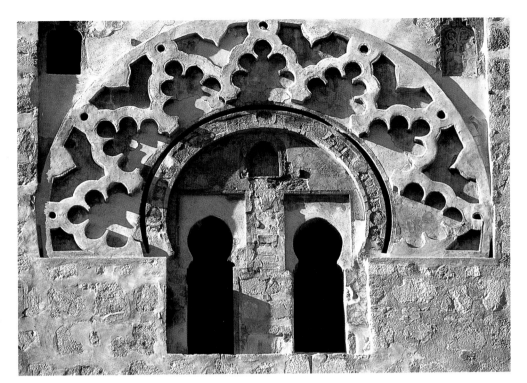

KOUTOUBIYA MOSQUE

The red stone minaret of the Koutoubiya
Mosque is over 70 metres high. The harmony
of its proportions is in keeping with Almohad
canons (five heights for one width)
and served as a model for the Giralda
in Seville and the Hassan Tower in Rabat.

KOUTOUBIYA MOSQUE

The walls of the mosque are a skilful
combination of different ornamental features:
arabesques in relief, finely carved arcatures
and floral and epigraphic motifs.

The plan is T-shaped, each of the seven bays being surmounted by a dome, while the stalactites decorating the arch of the axial nave prepare the worshipper for the sumptuous ornamentation of the *mihrab*. In the rest of the prayer-room, the smooth arches are horseshoe-shaped and clearly pointed. The transversal arches are multifoiled, while those perpendicular to the *qibla* are lanceolate. The pillars of the prayer-room, made of brick covered with plaster, open up surprising perspectives. The rectangular courtyard, in the middle of which stands a circular pond, is surrounded on two of its sides by galleries and prolonged on its northern side by triangular porticoes. The interior of the Koutoubiya, painted white throughout and decorated with strict geometrical forms, has a distinguished, almost austere, sobriety when compared with the ornamentation met with in Almoravid buildings.

The minaret of the Koutoubiya, towering 70 metres above the city, served as a model for that of the Giralda in Seville. Each of its outside walls, built with pink quarry stones from the Gueliz, has its own cunning arrangement of floral designs, epigraphs, festooned arches and faience-work friezes. The interior of the minaret consists of superimposed rooms around which a gently sloping ramp winds its way up to the turret landing. According to legend, the four bronze globes surmounting the minaret were originally made of pure gold melted down from the jewellery offered by one of al Mansour's wives after breaking the fast at Ramadan. (The largest sphere, it should be borne in mind, is two metres in diameter.)

The mosque of the kasbah was the work of the Almohad sovereign Yakoub al Mansour. Begun around 1190, it is remarkable for a very fine minaret which rivals in beauty that of the Koutoubiya. Several times redesigned, the mosque, though it has lost its original ornamentation, is a classic example of monumental Hispano-Mauresque architecture.

KASBAH MOSQUE
The mosque of the kasbah is
in the classical tradition, like that of
the Koutoubiya, and is decorated with
a magnificent network of arabesques
and turquoise-coloured glazing.

KOUTOUBIYA MOSQUE
A recently restored band of green glazed faience
tiling surrounds the top part of the minaret.
The turret is surmounted by four spheres
of gilded copper, the largest of which
is two metres in diameter.

The mosque, which is 80 metres long, consists of a T-shaped prayer-room and five open inner courtyards decorated with fountains and ponds. The organization of the architectural masses, the balancing of volumes and the alternation of solids and hollows and light and shadow show an Andalusian influence. The oratory has eight perpendicular naves and two bays, to which should be added a lateral nave running along the wall of the *qibla* and surmounted by three domes decorated with *moukarnas*. Note the remarkable Umayyad capitals supporting on three small columns of jasper the prayer niche of the *mihrab*, and the thirteenth-century *minbar* in carved wood inlaid with ivory. The exceptionally high roofs rest on multifoiled or pointed arches, themselves supported by gigantic pillars.

The powerful silhouette of the minaret, built like all Almohad minarets to a square plan, dominates the north-west corner of the prayer-room. Stripped of ornament all the way up to the sanctuary roof, and soberly decorated thereafter, it is surrounded by a green glazed tile frieze. A magnificent network of interlacing relief designs covers the greater part of its four sides. Its turret is surmounted by three famous copper globes, known since the sixteenth century as "the golden apples".

KOUTOUBIYA MOSQUE

The prayer-room of the Koutoubiya is one of the largest in the Moslem West and can accommodate some 20,000 worshippers. Its sixteen naves are supported by a suite of unadorned white arcades.

BEN YOUSSEF MOSQUE

This aerial view gives an idea of the size of the mosque, situated in the north part of the medina. The mosque commemorates another great saint of Marrakesh, the devout Sidi Youssef ben Ali.

MAUSOLEUM OF SIDI BEL ABBES

The sanctuary of the patron saint of the city, who is particularly revered by tradesmen, farmers and the blind.

The Tomb of the Saints

The city prides itself on its seven saints, the cult of which it celebrates with fervour in the mausoleums dedicated to them. The phenomenon has its roots in the mystical effervescence derived from Sufism which spread through the country between the fifteenth and seventeenth centuries. During the Merinid reign, to round off the conversion of the Berbers to Islam and combat the influx of Christian beliefs, the Sufis often led discussions in *zaouiyas* where, in opposition to the official *madrasas*, they expounded and extolled the lives of the saints. The legend of the seven saints, which can be found throughout the Maghrib and may be compared to the Christian myth of the seven sleepers of Ephesus, found fertile soil in Marrakesh. At the suggestion of Moulay Ismaïl, it gave rise to what is probably the most famous religious procession in the whole of Islam – so much so that, in everyday speech, the expression "seven men" has become synonymous with Marrakesh. The devotional route follows a fixed path through the medina, running south-west to south-east and passing through the north in the same direction as the pilgrims round the Kaaba at Mecca. It begins on the Tuesday and ends the following Monday, each day being reserved for a *wali*. Prayers, salutations, psalm-singing and the giving of alms accompany the followers throughout the procession.

MAUSOLEUM OF SIDI BEL ABBES

The ornamentation of the porched entranceway leading to the tomb of the saint is a remarkably delicate piece of work composed of several horizontal bands of chiselled plaster. The epigraphic frieze contains a *sura* from the Koran: "Only God is invincible".

The most revered of the seven is Sidi bel Abbès, the patron saint of the city. Born in 1130 at Ceuta, this itinerant preacher was remarked by al Mansour, who invited him to come and teach in the medina, a duty for which he forsook his vocation as a hermit. He was above all known as a patron of the blind, by whom he is especially revered to this day. He died in 1205, but it wasn't until 1605 that the Saadian sultan Abou Faris built a mausoleum in his name which has since been the object of special attention on the part of every sovereign and, in 1988, was renovated by King Hassan II. The sanctuary comprises a mosque, a *hammam*, a ritual slaughterhouse, latrines, a refuge for the blind and a cemetery. The mausoleum itself consists of a small patio and a funeral chamber the walls of which are decorated with *zillij* and stained-glass windows and surmounted by a painted wooden dome. The sepulchre is a rather squat structure decorated with glazed tiling and covered with a rug beside which pilgrims come to pray, calling on the saint for aid, protection and salvation.

Another saint, Sidi Youssef ben Ali, who though afflicted with leprosy remained unshaken in his faith right up to his death in 1196, has a building all to himself. The mosque of Ben Youssef, as it is called, is of Almoravid origin and was the main sanctuary of the medina for more than four centuries until the Mouassin Mosque was built. Only the name of its founder, the Almoravid sovereign Al ben Youssef, indicates the origin of this imposing edifice. The mosque underwent alterations and repairs in the sixteenth century, then again at the beginning of the nineteenth century, so that virtually nothing remains of the original building. The prayer-room, which is somewhat austere, has eleven naves and three bays and is covered in the Alouite style by twin-sloping roofs set parallel to the walls of the *qibla*. The roofing is supported by massive rectangular or square pillars surmounted by pointed horseshoe arches that have a certain charm. In keeping with local tradition, the ceilings are in painted wood and finely decorated by the craftsmen of Marrakesh. The rectangular courtyard is covered with *zillij* and ornamented with a beautiful ribbed marble basin. Two pairs of naves run along each side, culminating in a minaret on one side, and on the other, a dome. The monumental, 40-metre-high minaret is very fine and dominates the centre of the old imperial city.

Apart from these important devotional centres, the cult of the saints is also celebrated in the traditional feast (*moussem*), which each year gives rise to a lavish display of piety, sacrificial offerings and eloquence in which poets, singers and musicians hymn the praises of the guardians of the city. The Marrakchis, many of whom are still affiliated to a brotherhood or spiritual order, flock to the *moussem* in great numbers.

MAUSOLEUM OF THE SAADIAN PRINCES
Built in the sixteenth century by Ahmed al Mansour, the mausoleum
of the Saadian Princes contains the sepulchres of members of the Saadian dynasty.
The main building consists of three rooms: the *mihrab* room,
the room of the twelve columns and the room of the three niches.

The architectural complex designed to receive the tombs of the Saadian sovereigns is one of the architectural glories of that dynasty. A cemetery during the Almohad period, then later the necropolis of the Merinid sultan Abou al Hassan, it only acquired its present form at the end of the sixteenth century. A first edifice housed the tomb of Prince Mohammed al Cheikh, buried in 1557, the probable date which this royal necropolis was inaugurated. It was built by the sovereign Moulay Abdellah, who was himself laid to rest there in 1574. The second and smaller of the two buildings was certainly built by the great Ahmed al Mansour (died 1603), who, after burying his mother Lalla Massaouda there, was buried there in his turn, as were his three successors. In 1669, the sultan Moulay Ismaïl pulled down all the Saadian buildings in the kasbah to raze them from the memory of the capital, but, out of respect for the dead, left this sanctuary intact, while walling up the main entrance.

Surrounded by enormous high walls, for centuries the two buildings were completely forsaken by the outside world and protected against damage as a result. It was almost by chance that the department of Fine Arts and Historical Monuments "uncovered" them in 1917, while flying over the city. The two mausoleums, of average dimensions, are built in an oblong, open space surrounded by trees and flowers that is a haven of calm in the midst of a noisy, bustling kasbah.

The smaller of the two buildings, which is square-shaped with a roof of green tiles, consists of a room in which a small chapel, the *koubba* of Lalla Massaouda, is set, along with two loggias that look for all the world like miniature replicas of the pavilions of the Al Karaouyin Mosque. Their porticoes, with their double columns of white marble and epigraphic, cedar-wood lintels, have a certain refinement. The ceiling of this first mausoleum is formed by a marvellous dome of painted stalactites, and the niche in which the tomb is placed is decorated with alveoli. The delicacy of the craftsmanship, the value of the materials employed and the strong light with which the chapel is flooded make the lavish ornamentation very pleasing to the eye.

The larger of the two sanctuaries consists of a suite of three funeral chambers and appears to have been modelled on the Rawda in Granada. The central room, supported by twelve columns made with that famous Carrara marble that could be exchanged against its weight in sugar, houses beneath a black tombstone the remains of the great sovereign Moulay Ahmed al Mansour, surrounded by his male descendants. The lower part of the walls is entirely covered with magnificent faience tiling decorated with elegant, interlacing polygonal designs and crowned with

MAUSOLEUM OF THE SAADIAN PRINCES

Every conceivable architectural and ornamental device has been employed here. The Alouite sovereign Moulay Ismaïl was so impressed by the building that he decided not to destroy it; instead, he had it sealed off in 1677 by an impenetrable wall which helped protect the building until it was rediscovered in 1917.

two Koranic friezes, while the upper area is richly ornamented with stucco-work. The ceiling consists of a painted and gilded carved wooden dome adorned with stalactites and supported by lavishly decorated arches. Stucco stalactites are everywhere, sometimes adorning the arcades, sometimes suspended above the capitals; shaped like honeycombs, their craftsmanship is similar to that of carved ivory.

The eastern room is an oratory divided into three naves and three bays by four columns of white marble. The *mihrab*, with its pointed arch, is decorated with stalactites and rests on four marble semi-colonnettes. The last of the three rooms is rectangular in shape and lit by two square openings in the ceiling. The sumptuousness of its ornamentation, like the three finely decorated niches set into its west wall, serves to throw into relief the tombs of the wives and children of the Saadian princes. Each tomb is marked on the ground by a narrow gravestone (*mqabriya*) of ivory-coloured Italian marble. The finest of these are carved with a filigree of inscriptions and reserved for the tombs of the most prestigious Saadian sovereigns, of certain members of their family and even of the Alouite sovereign Moulay Yazid (1790-1792). A far cry from the asceticism of the Almohads, the funerary art adopted by the Saadians is one of great pomp and magnificence.

Situated in the north of the medina, the Ben Youssef *Madrasa*, founded in the fourteenth century then entirely rebuilt by the Saadian sovereign Moulay Abdellah al Ghalib in 1564, is an equally remarkable piece of work. In constructing one of the largest and most beautiful *madrasas* in the Maghrib, this builder-prince hoped to heal the wounds of Marrakesh, restore its prestige as imperial capital and endow the city with a monument that would express his piety and, at the same time, leave a mark on posterity. His *madrasa* was the most important Koranic university in the Maghrib.

Construction was carried out in a single bound and impresses one by its fine proportions and remarkable symmetry and coherence. The ground-plan of this huge, one-storied edifice is almost square. Marble and mosaic, carved cedar-wood and stucco, answer one another in a happy marriage. The main entrance, which consists of a finely carved door with heavy panels and a cedar-wood lintel carved with Andalusian script, gives onto a long corridor dimly lit by embrasures made in the cunningly wrought, painted wooden ceiling and leading on to the staircase and the passage into the courtyard.

The entranceway to this charming patio is placed on the same axis as a huge rectangular pond, the door of the prayer-room and the *mihrab*,

BEN YOUSSEF MADRASA
Like the Merinid *madrasas* of Fez,
the Ben Youssef *Madrasa* makes
harmonious use of *zillij*, wood and stucco.

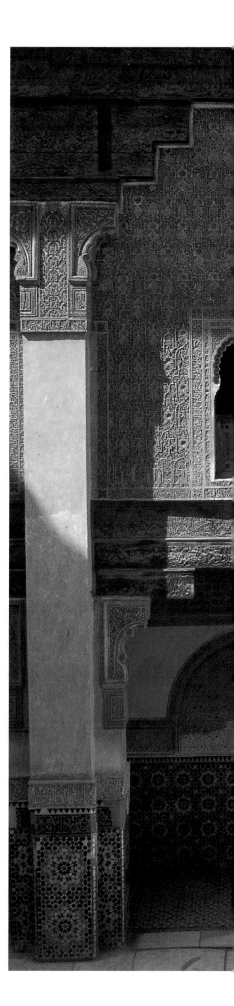

BEN YOUSSEF MADRASA

The Ben Youssef *Madrasa* is laid out on traditional lines: to either side of a central courtyard two galleries supported by pillars and consoles of carved wood contain cells for students. On the ground floor are rooms for study and prayer.

104 MARRAKESH, THE CITY OF THE SEVEN SAINTS

BEN YOUSSEF MADRASA

Small inner courtyards let light in from outside.
The ornamental repertoire handed down by earlier dynasties
is magnificently represented. There are also typically Saadian features,
such as the *mihrab* of the prayer-room, all but indistinguishable
from that found in the mausoleum of the Saadian princes.

dividing the building exactly in two. The oblong courtyard is spacious, well-lit and decorated with great skill. Its white marble flagstones are replaced in the galleries by polychrome *zillij*. The galleries running along the north and south sides are supported by massive pillars over the capitals of which are placed delicately carved wooden lintels. On the upper floor built over the two galleries can be found small cells, some hundred in all, originally used to lodge students, the small traceried windows of which overlook the patio, filtering the light within. The outer walls of the prayer-room and the main entrance are richly ornamented. All the walls are tiled along their lower edges with polychrome *zillij*, which likewise adorn the pillars of the courtyard, while the upper areas are composed of rectangular panels of sculpted plaster decorated with trompe-l'oeil doors and pelmet arches. The whole is crowned by very stylish corbelling and topped by the usual glazed green tiles.

At the far end of the courtyard is the prayer-room, rectangular in shape and divided into three parts by a double row of marble columns. The *mihrab* opposite the door to the prayer-room is decorated with finely carved colonnettes inscribed with verses from the Koran and has attractively ornamented windows.

Those ground-floor cells that are deprived of daylight from the main courtyard are organized around seven smaller courtyards reached by a corridor built round the main patio. The plan of the upper floor is virtually identical to that of the ground floor, but also includes narrow latrines equipped with small wash basins and fountains.

In function and structure, as well as in architecture and ornamentation, the *Madrasa* Ben Youssef is reminiscent of Merinid *madrasas*, particularly that of Bou Inania in Fez. Its quiet majesty makes up for the

simplicity of its plan and ornamentation; yet for all its architectural and aesthetic value, it is basically, like so many Saadian constructions, a continuation of the work of the Merinids.

Palaces and Gardens

After being swept to power at the battle of the Three Kings on August 4, 1578, Ahmed al Mansour had a huge official palace built alongside his harem and private apartments. Destined for important receptions and official audiences, Al Badi, as it is called, would enable the sultan's subjects and missions from abroad to admire the luxury with which the sovereign was surrounded. The building, on which his reputation is founded, was also designed to wipe out any memory of the work done by the great dynasties of the past. The site chosen for the palace was an abandoned Almohad garden in the north-east of the kasbah. Work began in December 1578 and, according to the chroniclers, was only completed sixteen years later, circa 1593-1594. According to the Koran, Al Badi ("the Incomparable") is one of the 99 names of God. The name has proved extremely popular in the history of the Moslem dynasties; one of the pavilions of the palace of Cordoba, as well as a garden laid out in Bougie by the Hammadids, bear this name.

The overall layout of the palace, which is highly formal, is modelled on the architecture of Granada, as is its style of ornamentation. The palace, however, was designed as much by engineers as by architects. To irrigate the gardens, large ponds were installed above ground level, obliging the builders to place the main rooms of the palace over brick arcades so that they would be at the same level as the water. Inside the building is a huge rectangular courtyard with a pond in the centre. To either side of the pond, two rectangular flower beds, once filled with flowers and trees, are divided into squares set round with paths of polychrome *zillij*. Four ponds situated at each of the four corners complete the symmetry of the courtyard. An imposing fountain consisting of two basins placed one above the other creates a feeling of harmony and quiet. On each side of the courtyard stands a monumental pavilion with green-tiled domes, an arrangement that calls to mind the architecture of the Court of the Lions in the Alhambra Palace in Granada.

Al Badi was originally protected by high walls on which four angle-towers had been built and of which no trace remains today. The palace, in fact, the sheer ostentation and luxury of which was hymned by every visitor and chronicler, was only used for royal receptions for three-quarters of a century, at which point Moulay Ismaïl had the entire thing dismantled, using its marble, onyx, ivory, gold and precious woods to help build the imperial city of Meknes. The whole operation, which was begun some time around 1696, took about ten years. Of this fabled palace straight out of the *Thousand and One Nights*, where marble vied with onyx and *zillij* with gold-leaf, all that remains is the basic structure, from which the ponds and gardens can just about be construed, and a few sections of brick and red clay walling.

In a very different spirit, the palace of al Bahia ("the Bright") is the work of two immensely powerful grand vizirs at the end of the nineteenth century. The first of its two complexes was built by Si Moussa, the grand vizir of the sultan Sidi Mohammed ben Abderrahman, the second by his son, Ahmed, called Ba Ahmed, the regent of Moulay Abdelaziz. The older of the two groups of buildings is fairly straightforward and is built round a marble-paved courtyard in which can be found two star-shaped ponds and a large, rectangular Moorish garden planted with cypress, orange, banana and jasmine.

To accommodate his large family and many servants, Ba Ahmed, to whom we owe the more recent of the two groups of buildings, ordered a huge palace to be built. Construction lasted seven years, as the contractor al Hajj Mohammed ben Makki al Mesfioui switched from one project to another to satisfy the whims of the regent. In other words, the finished whole corresponds to no particular plan. Lacking any pre-established scheme, al Bahia developed in haphazard fashion, as new plots of land or neighbouring houses were bought up and local thoroughfares disrupted. It consists of a series of buildings thrown up around large courtyards and patios filled with gardens and flowers, the whole thing extending over almost twenty acres. The most interesting of these buildings has a large rectangular courtyard paved with *zillij* and dazzling white marble flagstones and surrounded by a beautiful gallery with painted columns. Adorned with three fountains, this huge patio serves as an esplanade to an imposing main hall where there is an interesting wooden ceiling decorated with arabesques.

AL BADI PALACE

Even in ruins, the al Badi Palace makes a powerful impression with its harmonious lay-out, reminiscent of that of the Court of the Lions in Grenada. Pavilions and gardens were built around the huge rectangular pond.

AL BADI PALACE

Stripped of its precious materials by Moulay Ismaïl – fifty tons of Carrara marble are said to have been used for the decorations – this enormous palace still has some beautiful *zillij*-work mosaics left.

Designed for royal receptions, the Al Badi Palace
possessed not only living quarters and reception rooms
but all the attributes of a small city, including a mosque,
a tribunal and even an underground prison.

To build Al Bahia, Ba Ahmed called on the finest craftsmen in the land
and had rare materials brought in from other parts of the country :
marble from Meknes, cedar-wood from the Middle Atlas and faience
tiling from Tetouan. The palace of this enormously rich vizir is said to
have been stripped of its valuables only a few hours after his death, on
the orders of the jealous sultan Moulay Abdelazziz. Nevertheless, Al
Bahia still reflects some of its former glory and the spirit of the great
builders of old.

In the same period, Ba Ahmed's brother had another remarkable palace
built by the same team of craftsmen : Dar Si Saïd. Si Saïd, who was likewise a vizir, died just as the works were about to be completed. His beautiful home is a stone's throw from his brother's palace. Laid out on
traditional lines, with several courtyards and an Andalusian garden, the
palace is composed of several small patioed buildings arranged around a
larger, storied building. Nevertheless, it is smaller and less impressive
than al Bahia. The architecture and ornamentation draw on the artistic
heritage of the past, but show that crafts techniques were still very much
alive at the time. Polychrome *zillij*, marble fountains, delicately chiselled plaster and wooden ceilings and domes painted with geometrical
and floral designs catch the eye, giving the palace the elegance to which
this influential figure aspired. Part of the building currently houses the
Marrakesh Museum of Moroccan Arts.

AL BADI PALACE

This princely residence, which dates from the late nineteenth
century and took seven years to build, consists of a series
of lavishly decorated apartments on which the craftsmen
have brought to bear all the resources of their art.

In the north-west corner of the medina, near Bab Doukkala, is the Dar al Glaoui, the palace of the last pasha of Marrakesh, who played an important role both prior to and during the French Protectorate. A native of the Glaoua tribe, the pasha amassed an enormous personal fortune through his exactions, and a no less enormous fiefdom in the High Atlas. Built at the turn of the century, his palace is surrounded by high walls the colour of Marrakesh and consists of several lavishly decorated courtyards flanked by rooms adorned with *zillij*, stucco-work, painted wood and *moukarnas*; there is also a very beautiful Andalusian garden carefully planted with fruit-trees, shrubs and a dazzling array of richly-scented flowers. The palace was used to hold receptions that left their mark on the period and were renowned for their eccentricity. Part of the palace complex now houses a department of Morocco's Ministry of Cultural Affairs, the other part being used to receive foreign dignitaries.

In the west of the city, far from the bustle of the souks of the medina, can be found the splendid gardens of the Menara, their enormous olive-groves decorated with a large pond in which a delightful pavilion is reflected. Probably laid out in the twelfth century during the Almohad period and kept up by the Saadians, the gardens were redesigned by Moulay Mohammed ben Abderrahman (1859-1873), who rebuilt the pleasure pavilion, notable for its thick walls and brick corners and its traditional, pyramid-shaped roof overlaid with green tiles. The ground

DAR SI SAID PALACE

A door combining traditional
Hispano-Mauresque ornamentation
with motifs derived
from European naturalism.

DAR SI SAID PALACE

This handsome late-nineteenth-century
home now houses the Museum
of Moroccan Arts. Some of its rooms reveal
a falling-off in the quality of decorative
composition and a certain rigidity
in the execution of the carved designs.

DAR SI SAID PALACE

A pond and white marble basin add
a refreshing touch to this typically
Andalusian garden.

THE MENARA

This small Saadian pavilion, soberly refurbished,
stands on the edge of an enormous
reservoir fed by the Almoravid canalisation system.

Page 116
THE MENARA PAVILION
The garden façade
at the sunrise.

floor, with its four fat pillars, was for domestic use and is preceded by a three-vaulted loggia which overlooks the pond. On the first floor, a wide door with a rounded arch opens onto a large, north-facing balustered balcony. The fittings and interior decorations of the pavilion are very plain, since it was designed as part of a larger whole, in keeping with the ideal of a Moroccan imperial garden. From an aesthetic point of view, the Menara is an unqualified success. From the balcony, as from any opening in the pavilion, you find yourself gazing out onto a vast land-scape, spell-bound by the forms and colours of a carefully cultivated nature and the shadows and light thrown by this subdued architecture.

3. Meknes, the City of the Prince

| Pages 118-119

THE MEDINA

From left to right,
the minarets of the Zaytouna
Mosque, the Great Mosque
and the Nejjarin
and Tijani sanctuaries.

THE MEDINA

Girded round with high,
crenellated, yellow-ochre walls,
the tightly-knit terraces
of the medina leave very little
space free between them.

A vast, fertile plain, protected to the north by the massif of the Zerhoun, fields criss-crossed by streams and yielding an abundance of wheat, fruit and vegetables–in such a landscape, it would be impossible for Meknes to overlook its agricultural origins. Even if it wanted to, two facts would prevent it from doing so. The first is historical : only a few kilometres from the outskirts of town can be found the marvellous ruins of Volubilis, which in 40 BC was the capital of Mauritania Tingitana, a province that served as a granary for the Roman Empire. The second is its name : ever since the ninth century, it has been called Meknassa ez Zitoun ("Meknes of the olive trees"). Like Cinderella, though, this sleepy market-town exchanged its humble Berber dwellings for a more sumptuous attire. The oversized village turned into the Moroccan equivalent of Versailles. This was in the seventeenth century, the fairy-godmother being Moulay Ismaïl, a sultan of the Alouite dynasty. Even today, overflowing its triple ramparts and coupled with a modern city, Meknes is conscious of how much it owes to this megalomaniac admirer of Louis XIV. It is a city conjured from one man's dreams.

An Unfinished Dream

While the great cities of Fez and Marrakesh were built by princes to help convert their peoples to Islam and the Arab world and to guarantee military control and political stability, Meknes came into being independently of any dynastic will. Founded some time around the tenth century by the Meknassa, a Zanata Berber tribe that took advantage of the decline of the Idrissid Kingdom to invade the fertile plains of western Morocco, it originally consisted of a handful of unwalled market-towns huddled together around the Oued Boufekran in the northern Middle Atlas. It is a peaceful agricultural and fruit-bearing region, the prosperity of which is celebrated in the story-books of old. Each clan within the tribe had its own district, with its mosques, its *hammams* and all the different structures needed for a sedentary Moslem life. This easy-going, Mediterranean existence was to be disrupted by the arrival of the Almoravids.

The first Almoravid sovereign, Youssef ben Tachfin, took possession of Meknes some time around 1063. To establish firm control over the region, he built on the plateau, as was the practice almost everywhere in the Almoravid empire, a watchtower and a kasbah (a fortified city) that today form the district of Touta and which would gradually eclipse the old market-towns, bringing together all their inhabitants of importance. In 1145, after laying siege to it for several years, the Almohads conquered the town and in their turn sacked the greater part of it. A few years later, they ceased their exactions and integrated the city in their plans for extending the Hispano-Mauresque empire. Meknes developed according to an astonishing grid plan, enjoying the benefits of the peace proclaimed by the Almohads and the riches that changed hands over their vast territory. It also took advantage of its proximity to Fez and Andalusia to repopulate itself. The city attracted foreign traders and enjoyed an unprecedented period of demographic growth and an architectural boom. Sanctuaries and civil buildings went up inside its ramparts. This happy period of prosperity came to an end with the decline and fall of the Almohads. The devastation and pillaging wreaked on Morocco by Berber nomads and Hilalien Arabs (bedouins from Arabia) led to the withering of the countryside and the emptying of the cities; abandoned by their inhabitants, who had taken refuge within the walls of the new city, the ancient market-towns of Meknes became orchards once again.

The Merinids, who established their capital in Fez in 1244, did not neglect Meknes which, being situated nearby, allowed them to keep control of the fertile plains. To its traditional Hispano-Mauresque structure they added a kasbah in the southern part of the town, destined to house a governor, his officials and the army. Meknes now consisted, like all the imperial cities, of two entities separated by walls: a commercial town and a government town (later demolished by Moulay Ismaïl to make way for the palace of Dar al Kebira). To the Merinids we above all owe the *madrasa* of Bou Inania, twin sister to the *madrasa* of Fez.

THE RAMPARTS OF THE KASBAH

The ramparts of the kasbah are three deep, giving the town the appearance of a citadel.
Thousands of slaves, prisoners of war and Christian captives were employed to build them.
The best-preserved of the walls is the outer of the three, called "the wall of the wealthy".

PLACE LALLA AWDA

The Place Lalla Awda was built on the site
of the old *mechouar* where official ceremonies
were held. Behind the walls of the Dar
al Kebira Palace, is the Lalla Awda mosque,
the first sanctuary to be built by Moulay Ismaïl
and the only mosque in the royal city
in which sermons are delivered.

The waning of the Merinid dynasty in the early fifteenth century, and
the anarchy that resulted throughout the country, led to the decline of
Meknes, which was reduced to a dull provincial town. Despite its strategic position, it played only a minor political role under the two dynasties, Wattasid and Saadian, that succeeded the Merinids. Beauty fell into
a sleep that was to last for two centuries.

Her awakening, when it came, was all the more dramatic. For now came
the reign – that was to last fifty-five years – of the Alouite sultan, Moulay
Ismaïl who, after being appointed governor of Meknes by his brother,
became sultan of the Alouite dynasty on the latter's death in 1672. All
kinds of legends surround his life. Portrayed as a cruel man who person-
ally cut the heads off condemned men, enjoyed the pleasures of the flesh
and had a harem composed of hundreds of wives as well as numerous
offspring, Moulay Ismaïl was, in reality, an absolute monarch, the founder of modern Morocco with an authority that extended as far as
Senegal as well as the "inventor" of Morocco's first professional army.
The latter was made up of a military corps of black slaves, the *abid*,
out-and-out mercenaries devoted to his cause, whose presence at his
side – 150,000 men at the height of his power – meant he was no longer

dependent on the loyalty of the tribes. Moulay Ismaïl installed barracks in strategically placed kasbahs, creating a network of staging-posts – 76 small forts, still used to this day – which guaranteed him complete surveillance of the country. A shrewd statesman, he organized the *makh-zen* and modernised the administration. On the international plane, he succeeded in taking back Tangier from the English, and Mahdia and Larache from the Spaniards. A contemporary of Louis XIV, he remains the most famous of the Alouite kings.

Moulay Ismaïl chose Meknes as his capital the moment he came to the throne, sanctioning Fez and Marrakesh in this way for their rebellious spirit and giving a new direction to the destiny of the city, which, for the first time in its history, was laying claim to the title of imperial capital. His decision betrays the resolve of a strategist and great sovereign to control the rebellious Berbers of central Morocco, and doubtless the need to build a city of his own. The man proved to be a passionate buil-der who could not content himself with living in one of his predeces-sors' capitals, even after he had rebuilt it. He needed a town after his own image, one that would preserve for posterity the mark of his tastes and

BAB AL MANSOUR

Commissioned by Moulay Ismaïl from a renegade Christian, Bab Al Mansour was the official entrance to the royal city. Its horse-shoe arch is flanked by two arcaded bastions, a structure not commonly found in the architecture of Moroccan gateways.

ideas. Meknes, moreover, was enviably placed strategically and situated in a very rich area; the abundance of water and the fertility of its soil influenced the sovereign's choice.

With unrivalled fervour, the king embarked on a series of monumental building projects for the capital that he would pursue without let through his entire life. A whole host of contractors, masons, navvies and craftsmen specialised in every conceivable field of art, along with work-men drawn from the ranks of common-law prisoners, black slaves and Christian captives interned in Meknes (to say nothing of whole tribes enrolled by force) were put to work on the gigantic building-site that Meknes had become. Craftsmen were borrowed from the other great cities of Morocco, led off by force to work for Moulay Ismaïl. The sovereign spared no effort, watching over the progress of the works, setting an example, pickaxe in hand, flogging and punishing with great cruelty less zealous workers, even to the point of death. His impatience was great and his projects subject to constant modification. As his ambition and power grew, and with them the needs of his administration and army, he would order this or that building, that had only just gone up, to be pulled down and replaced by another. The entire kingdom was requi-sitioned to help build these enormous palaces and walls. Every historic site in the country was plundered for materials, particularly if it had been built by the Saadians; the consequences this had for the Al Badi Palace in Marrakesh were dramatic.

In the space of a few years, Meknes was transformed. To build the palace complexes, ponds, gardens, stables – said to have been able to accommo-date 12,000 horses – granaries, arsenals and forts for his guards, the sove-reign ordered the Merinid kasbah to be pulled down, along with an old neighbourhood of the medina adjoining it to the south. The space cleared in this way has been known ever since as the Sahat al Hedim ("Debris Square"), in remembrance of the enormous heaps of rubble the inhabitants were forced to clear away. He also had the old walls of the city pulled down and replaced by new ones pierced by imposing gate-ways like Bab al Khemis, Bab Berdayin and Bab al Jedid. As testimony to his great piety, the commercial town was furnished with religious buil-dings, such as the mosques of Bab Berdayin, Sidi Said, Bouazza and the Zaytouna, largely modelled on the Saadian constructions of Marrakesh; nor did he overlook the saints worshipped in Meknes, as can be seen from the tombs of Sidi Ahmed al Chabli, Sidi Youssef ben Cherif and Sidi Abdellah al Qasri.

In addition, Moulay Ismaïl, like his predecessors in Fez and Marrakesh, indulged in large-scale city development by creating a *mellah*. The latter is not tucked away in the royal city, as it is in the other imperial cities,

BAB AL MANSOUR

The bay and the two bastions are sumptuously decorated with a network of openwork arabesques and *zillij* designs with a predominance of green.

but on the west side of the commercial district, next to the garden district Madinat al Riyad where the dignitaries of the *makhzen* live.

Fifty years of non-stop labour were insufficient to complete Moulay Ismaïl's architectural works, the gigantic scale of which is said to have been fuelled, among other things, by his admiration for Louis XIV. The reports brought back by the embassy he had dispatched to the court of the Sun King filled him with so much enthusiasm that he even requested the hand of the French sovereign's daughter, Anne-Marie de Bourbon, in marriage. Though his eagerness to see them finished often militated against the sultan's projects, they left their mark on the age; in a period when craftsmanship was on the decline he gave new momentum to the art of building, and to palace architecture in particular.

After his death, the *abid* sparked off a palace revolution that was to last twenty years, plunging the kingdom into anarchy and civil war. Devastating the region of Fez and Meknes, the mountain Berbers also took part in the general uprising.

The architectural fervour of the reign of Moulay Ismaïl all but vanished from Meknes, despite the buildings later put up under the reign of Moulay Mohammed ben Abdellah (1757-1790). After that, the Alouite sovereigns moved their residence, sometimes to Fez, sometimes to Marrakesh. In the late eighteenth century, the medina acquired more or less the shape and size it has today. The sovereigns who ruled over the country in the nineteenth century, Moulay Abderrahman and Moulay al Hassan (1873-1894), kept up, in somewhat desultory fashion, the palaces of the kasbah which today form Dar al Makhzen, while the other buildings were left in the unfinished state in which they had found them. There will soon be little left of the works carried out by Moulay Ismaïl.

At the turn of the century, Meknes suffered the same ups and downs as the rest of Morocco. In 1911, the French general, Moinier, arrived in the old walled city. The latter now exists side by side, as in Fez and Marrakesh, with a new city built on the opposite bank of the Oued Boufekrane according to the plan laid out by Louis Hubert Lyautey, who took care to preserve the old imperial city. The Meknes of today is a many-faceted and motley agglomeration : Berbers from the Middle Atlas, Arabs from the plains and Andalusians and Jews from the *mellah* constitute the life-blood of a city that, though it has undoubtedly lost the sparkle it had in the seventeenth century, still remains the fifth largest city of the kingdom and a bustling economic centre in the midst of a thriving agricultural region.

BAB AL KHEMIS

Likewise built by Moulay Ismaïl, Bab Al Khemis was the main gateway
to the "city of the amber garden" and the *mellah* (the Jewish quarter).
Its ornamentation is reminiscent of that on Merinid gateways :
lobed arcatures and floral designs cut out on faience.

BAB BERDAIN

Situated away from the medina, Bab Berdaïn
owes its name to the makers of pack-saddles
who held their market there. It is built
on the same plan as all the city's gateways,
with projecting towers and a richly decorated
ogival bay.

Majesty and Excess

At first sight, the medina, the greater part of which is enclosed within
large, high walls with a rampart walk surmounted by earthworks, looks
like a sturdy fortress. The surrounding walls, shaped like an irregular
polygon and consolidated at key points by watchtowers, are three deep.
Built with *pisé* using medieval construction techniques, they are up to
three metres deep and fifteen metres high in places. Their outline, perfectly adapted to the irregularities of the terrain, forms a zigzag that
takes in the medina and the *mellah* to the north. Their forbidding
appearance and their resistance to military attack mark an advance on
Andalusian and Almohad defence works. Inside the walls, Meknes is
made up, like all the imperial cities, of two disproportionate entities laid
out in a somewhat motley fashion. The medina proper, condensed over
a small area, is organized like a maze; the kasbah, on the other hand,
spreads over a vast area that is partly uninhabited and was originally surrounded along most of its perimeter by three ramparts designed to stop
cavalry, foot-soldiers and, in the last resort, any remaining intruders
who had managed to find their way in. The inner and outer walls are
still standing, but the second rampart has all but vanished. The buildings of the prince's city, themselves protected by high walls, were like

small citadels inside a larger fortress. Since the fortifications were concentric, openings had to be made to give access to the medina, the different districts and the palace complex. The town has dozens of gateways, some of which are extremely elegant, justifying Meknes's reputation as the "city of the beautiful gates".

The most monumental and prestigious of these gateways takes its name from the renegade Christian thought to have designed it, Bab Mansour al Eulj. It opens the ramparts of the kasbah that run along the northwest side of the medina, giving access to the Place Lalla Awda and the sumptuous palace, Dar al Kebira, built by Moulay Ismaïl. Bab al Mansour, begun by Moulay Ismaïl, was completed by his son. Its massive proportions make a very powerful impression and it has a classic double-stepped structure. The opening bay is crowned with a very slightly pointed horseshoe arch. It is above all its ornamentation, however, that compels our admiration. Pierre Loti compared it to a silky fabric, brocaded time and again and "draped over these ancient stones to break up the tedium of these high ramparts". The magnificent network of lozenge-shaped mouldings is combined with a very dense arrangement of floral designs, rosettes, horseshoe openings and tracery set against a background of green faience tiling. The two projecting side

BAB AL KHEMIS

A beautiful Kufic inscription ornaments the arch of Bab Al Khemis : "I am the fortunate gate, comparable in my glory to the full moon in the sky. I was built by Moulay Ismaïl. Fortune and prosperity are written on my brow. I am surrounded by happiness."

towers, each pierced at its base by two openings forming a loggia, are supported by Corinthian columns thought to have come from the Al Badi Palace in Marrakesh.

Of the five main gateways to the medina, mention should be made of that to the north-west, Bab al Khemis, the "gate of the Thursday market", one of the most beautiful of those built by Moulay Ismaïl. Now lost in a sea of more recent constructions, it was once the main gateway to the Madinat al Ryad al Anbari ("the city of the amber gardens") and the *mellah*, situated in the seventeenth century on land belonging to a Jewish physician who had cured one of the princesses. The garden city, built to house the Arab warrior tribe of the Oudaya and, at a later date, the dignitaries of the court, was pulled down in 1729 by Moulay Abdellah and the mellah moved elsewhere. This monumental gateway, fitted between two square towers, has a slightly pointed horseshoe arch surrounded by two relief arch mouldings. It is decorated with black spandrels bordered by green *zillij* and adorned with interlacing floral motifs, ornamental designs derived from the famous scalloped mouldings found on the oldest Almohad gates and Kufic script. The message contained in the epigraphic frieze gives a good idea of the atmosphere during the reign of Moulay Ismaïl: "I am the fortunate gate, comparable in my glory to the full moon in the sky. I was built by Moulay Ismaïl. Fortune and prosperity are written on my brow. Happiness is all round me". And also: "I am the gate that is open to all peoples, whether from the West or from the East".

STREETS IN THE MEDINA

Away from the bustle of the souks, the narrow streets of the medina are as peaceful and secret as those of Fez or Marrakesh. Only the occasional overhanging roof or ornamented doorway hint at more sumptuous interiors.

The Place al Hedim is the starting-point for any stroll through the medina, which has the same plan as all the imperial cities and was designed in the Middle Ages in the form of a maze. It is organized around two main thoroughfares that meet at right angles at the Al Mansour Palace, the first running north to south and linking Bab Berdaïn to the spiritual and economic centre of the city, the second leading off from Bab Berrima in the west and likewise culminating in the centre. Secondary roads, onto which numerous blind alleys have been grafted, link it to the residential districts. In keeping with custom, each district is given over to a particular class of activities from the centre to the periphery, the latter being reserved for poor people, countryfolk and foreigners. At the centre of the medina can be found the Great Mosque, the Merinid *Madrasa* Bou Inania and the beautiful *kissariya*, formerly the fabrics market. The souks consist of small boutiques placed side by side (some covered, some open-air) and specialised *fondouks* occupying several streets. Though Meknes has no great crafts tradition, its narrow streets are by no means lacking in interest. In the vaulted rooms of Bab al Jedid, for example, musical instruments are sold. The Bezzazin Souk is made up of basket-weavers and fabric merchants, while the Rue des Serraïra is reserved for coal-merchants and ironworkers. In the Rue des Armuriers can be found the souk for rock-salt, along with sawmills and blacksmiths' forges. The road leading off from Bab Berrima is used for the joiners' souk (al Nejjarin) and the coppersmiths' and cobblers' souk (al Sebbat). Further on, next to the grain market, is the El Ghezara Souk

STREETS IN THE MEDINA
The streets belong
to the local inhabitants,
who look after their upkeep
and sometimes use them
as an extension of their homes.

AL HADI BEN AISSA ZAOUIYA

The Al Hadi ben Aïssa *Zaouiya* is named after the saint who, according to legend, changed olive leaves into gold. Its green-tiled, pyramid-shaped roof and minaret are signs of the mausoleum's prestige; each year it attracts crowds of worshippers for the anniversary of the Prophet's birth.

FANTASIA

The cavalry displays held during the *moussem*
celebrate traditional equestrian skills.
Costumed riders simulate
a military attack with a salvo of gunfire.

THE ROYAL STABLES

A great rider, Moulay Ismaïl had huge stables built,
a monumental suite of twenty-two arcades
designed to house a stud farm
of several hundred horses but today in ruins.

The Kasbah of Moulay Ismaïl

The imperial city of Moulay Ismaïl is huge, more than four times the size of the medina. Above all, its high double walls with their numerous corridors and imposing gateways make it a mighty citadel comparable to the fortified *ksour* of the Atlas. It encloses palaces and institutional buildings–themselves protected by sturdy ramparts–as well as esplanades, ponds and enormous gardens. There are three palace complexes in all: Dar al Kebira, Dar al Madrasa and Ksar al Mhanncha.

Dar al Kebira ("the Great House") was the first palace complex built by the sovereign some time around 1672 in the south-east of the medina on what was probably the site of the old Almohad kasbah. Separated from the medina by double walls and the great Place al Hedim, Dar al Kebira presented a rather confused appearance, being composed of some twenty buildings known as *ksour*. Twelve hundred eunuchs guarded the entrances. Each palace was originally made up of a harem, reception rooms, *hammams*, kitchens, shops, ovens, mosques and so on, and was reached through a maze of open-air or partially vaulted corridors running between the high walls. The complex likewise contained an isolated pavilion, Koubba al Kayatin, also known as the "Ambassadors' Pavilion", which was originally used for receptions. An underground prison, Habs Qara ("the Prison of the Christians") was situated south-west of the first wall.

Dar al Kebira has since been abandoned and is now a field of ruins where poor citizens have set up makeshift homes; part of the old centre of the imperial city, however, has been converted into a district comparable to those of the medina. Only a very few buildings, such as the

PRISON OF THE CHRISTIANS

In addition to its vast palace complexes,
the kasbah of Moulay Ismaïl had underground corridors where
Christians captured by the sovereign's pirates were imprisoned.
These prisoners were then put to work
on the numerous building projects of the capital.

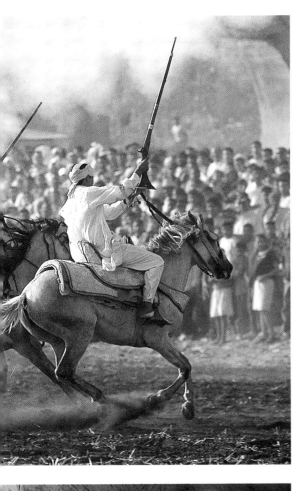

mosque of Lalla Awda and the mausoleum of Moulay Ismaïl, have survived the ups and down of history and the erosions of time.

The second group of buildings was the Dar al Madrasa palace ("the School Palace"). Situated south of Dar al Kebira and surrounded by ramparts of *pisé*, it was made up of living quarters, kitchens and *hammams*, as well as a belvedere, prayer-room, minaret and slaughter-house (all built round patios) and a large garden. A whole string of royal homes were built to house the sovereign and his wives and concubines. All that remains today is ruins.

Unlike the other royal complexes, which were built according to no particular plan, Ksar al Mhanncha ("the Palace of the Maze") is almost rectangular in shape, well-organized and broken up by walls and raised walkways into eight fairly similar parts. It is surrounded by ramparts that are reinforced with bastions and surmounted by a rampart walk on its south side. In the middle of the front wall is a monumental gateway, Bab al Makhzen, built during the reign of Moulay al Hassan in 1888. The Bab al Makhzen corridor leads to a large courtyard lined with porticoes and dominated by the silhouette of a mosque probably built by Moulay Sliman (1792-1822) and heavily inspired by Ottoman architecture. In front of the mosque stands a menagerie, Duwayriyat al Sbaa ("the Lion House"), and behind it to the north a small building originally destined for the Treasury. Complicated winding paths lead to Duwayriyat al Nasr ("the Little House of Victory"), an official building with galleries and a sort of throne room. Another monumental inner gateway, Bab Abid al Dar ("the Door of the Servants of the House"), furnished with sentry-boxes, leads to the large main courtyard. Rather sober-looking pavilions have been built in the middle of each of the north-, east- and west-facing walls. As in the Saadian palace of al Badi, there is a magnificent Andalusian garden, Gharsat al Rukham ("the Marble Garden"), covering a mere sixth of the parkland separating the main courtyard and Dar al Madrasa. North-east of Ksar al Mhanncha can be found a final building, Ksar al Chems ("the Palace of the Sun"), which, though less elegant than the main courtyard, is far more sophisticated from an architectural and ornamental point of view.

Ksar al Mhanncha today houses the royal palace, Dar al Makhzen. Laid out rather better than the other palaces of the kasbah, but less elegant than the great masterpieces of thirteenth- and sixteenth-century Hispano-Mauresque architecture, it unites all the traditional styles of Moroccan decorative art; and, though it has been modified over the centuries, notably by Moulay Abderrahman and Moulay al Hassan, it remains the architectural embodiment of the will of a single prince.

Moulay Ismaïl himself chose his last resting place. His mausoleum, set apart from the other buildings of the kasbah, was probably constructed alongside an already existing tomb, that of Morocco's great sixteenth-century saint, poet and mystic, Sidi Abderrahman al Majdoub. Though no description of the original tomb has come down to us, it is certain to have been the object of far-reaching modifications during the reigns of

MAUSOLEUM OF MOULAY ISMAIL

Situated in the old Dar al Kebira palace, the mausoleum has a pyramid-shaped roof of green tiles surmounted by four copper spheres and a monumental gateway, conferring on it the importance of a holy site.

BAB AL MAKHZEN

Built by Moulay al Hassan I in the late nineteenth century, the gateway is now the main entrance to the Royal Palace.

Moulay Ismaïl's son and successor Moulay Mohammed al Dehbi (1727-1729) and, in the twentieth century, King Mohammed V.

Situated to the south of the palace, the royal mausoleum runs between the second and third walls and has been adjusted to the shape of the two ramparts. Moulay Ismaïl's mausoleum is modelled directly on the Saadian tombs in Marrakesh, which were themselves based on Hispano-Mauresque architecture. With its suite of three chambers, its twelve columns and its central area reserved for the prince's remains, the lay-out of the funeral chamber is identical to that of the Saadians. Considered as a whole, however, the mausoleum is somewhat atypical, not least for its somewhat surprising siting of the *mihrab* in an uncovered patio and for certain irregularities of form. There is one amusing detail: the funeral chamber, which is covered with mats and contains the sepulchres of the sultan, his descendants and his wife Lalla Khouata, still displays the two clocks presented to Moulay Ismaïl by Louis XIV as consolation, it is said, for refusing him his daughter's hand in marriage.

MAUSOLEUM OF MOULAY ISMAIL

Though similar in plan to the burial places of the Saadian princes of Marrakesh, the mausoleum of Moulay Ismaïl is unusual for the soberness of the rooms leading to the sepulchres.

Page 154

MAUSOLEUM OF MOULAY ISMAIL

The funeral chambers in which the sovereign, his successors and his wife have been laid to rest are decorated along more traditional lines. The twelve Corinthian columns of the square gallery are believed to have come from the ruins of Volubilis.

4. Rabat, the Alouite Capital

THE KASBAH OF THE OUDAYA

Once an outpost in the holy
war against the Christians
of Spain, this twelfth-century
Almohad fortress today
encloses within its walls
a quiet district of
small white houses.

THE RAMPARTS OF THE OUDAYA

To the west, the ramparts built by Yakoub
al Mansour after his victory over Alfonso III
of Castille in 1195 are more than
five kilometres in length. Restored
in the seventeenth and eighteenth centuries
by the Mudejars and the Alouite sovereigns
they have retained their original outline.

Stretched peacefully along the south bank at the mouth of the Bou Regreg, where the wide, foam-capped waves of the Atlantic unfurl, lies the unpretentious and graceful city of Rabat – Rabat the Andalusian, Rabat the Holy. The city is a mixture of Mediterranean culture and oceanic longings; rising up before an infinite blue horizon, steeped in a boundless ocean and an azure sky, attached to its fertile green plains and nourished to the south by the river in which its remarkable landscape is reflected, its destiny is bound up with water. The unbroken lines of terraces, the courtyards and gardens, the minarets and domes which punctuate its architecture stand out against the ocean from which the city's wealth derives.

For all its charms, Rabat's geographical situation, facing the town of Salé, did not really single it out to become a capital. The somewhat oppressive dampness of the city, and its off-centre position on the west coast far from eastern Morocco and the Sahara, hardly spoke in its favour. The city occupies the extreme western tip of the great trail that runs along the corridor of Taza joining the fertile plain of the Gharb to the rest of the Berber world. It is doubtless for this reason that Rabat has never been as important as Fez or Marrakesh.

Rabat in History

The historical origins of Rabat are lost in the mists of time, or almost: the estuary of the Oued Bou Regreg is known to have been the site of Phoenician, then Carthaginian trading-posts, and vestiges have been found in Chella attesting to the existence of a settlement there in the third century BC. Rabat, at all events, was the Sala Colonia of Roman Mauritania during the reign of Trajan. Some time around the tenth

THE KASBAH OF THE OUDAYA

The Jamaa al Atiq Mosque built by
the Almohads in 1150 is the oldest mosque
in Rabat. Its minaret, restored in the eighteenth
century, towers over the surrounding houses
and the flat roof of an old bastion.

RAMPARTS OF THE KASBAH OF THE OUDAYA

In the east of the city, the crenellated
fortress walls conceal a charming Andalusian
garden, while in the distance can be
seen the Hassan Tower and the celebrated
mausoleum of Mohammed V.

century, the Zanata Berbers used it as their base camp for expeditions against the heretical Khajarite Moslems, building a *ribat*, or fortified monastery, on the cliffs overlooking the south bank of the *oued*. The town would not only keep the name, but, for a long time, preserved the character of a city committed to the *jihad*, or holy war. This was the role assigned to it by the Almohad sovereign Abd el Moumen when he made it a place of assembly for the *mudjahidin*, or "fighters for the faith", trained to wage battle against the Christian armies in Spain and Tunisia, which had been overrun by the Normans. He converted the *ribat* into a kasbah, a fortified city equipped with a mosque and a palace, and, after winning back the major part of Andalusia, baptised it Ribat al Fath ("the camp of victory"). His grandson, Yakoub al Mansour, to celebrate his great victory over Alfonso VIII at Alarcos, built a fortified wall and a mosque in Rabat, of which all that remains today is the Hassan Tower. His plans to make the town into a great capital were cut short by his death, as was his dream of a timeless Moorish empire, which was permanently compromised after defeat at Las Novas de Tolosa in 1212. Though some attention was paid to the town by the Merinids, Rabat now went into a very long period of decline, and, by the sixteenth century, was reduced to some hundred or so houses.

It wasn't until 1609 that Rabat awoke from its slumbers. Driven out by Philip III, the last Moors of Spain, the Mudejars, found refuge in the

towns of the Maghrib, notably in Salé and Rabat. These Andalusians, who were also known as "Hornacheros" after the Spanish town of Hornachos, settled in the medina of Rabat named Salé-le-Neuf, in contrast to Salé-l'Ancien on the opposite bank of the river. Filled with the bitterness of exile and home-sick for the country they had forsaken, they soon found an original way of integrating themselves on Moroccan soil by becoming Barbary pirates who would ply back and forth between the Canary Islands and the English Channel, leaving a trail of terror in their wake among the English galleys returning from the Americas laden with silver and gold. They even ended up forming their own political organization, the Republic of the Two Shores, which lasted from 1627 to 1641. Independent from the Saadian dynasty in power at the time, it elected its own governor each year. The two medinas enjoyed a period of unprecedented wealth, being the rallying point for all the Barbary pirates from Tripoli to Algiers. Run-down buildings were rebuilt and there was even a school of piracy. The western powers would always prefer to negotiate, particularly after 1666 when the sultans took control of the buccaneers' activities, deriving substantial revenues from them in the form of taxes. The last act of piracy was carried out against an Austrian vessel in 1829. The following year, the French took possession of Algiers and put an end to the activities of the Barbary pirates.

If Rabat and Salé were not wholly neglected during the reign of Moulay Ismaïl, this was because they provided the sultan with money and, above

THE WALL OF THE KASBAH

The Mudejars driven out of Spain
in the seventeenth century updated
the city's defence works to keep pace
with the development of artillery.
This flat-roofed bastion near the entrance
to the kasbah, for example, was pierced
with openings to accommodate canons.

all, the Christian slaves needed to finish building Meknes. (A detachment of *abid* was permanently stationed in the Kasbah of the Oudaya for this purpose.) The town was accorded the status of imperial capital for the first time in the eighteenth century, during the reign of Mohammed ben Abdellah (1757-1790). On account of the uprisings and anarchy sweeping through the tribes of central Morocco, the trade route between Fez and Marrakesh now passed through Rabat. The Alouite sovereigns profited from this state of affairs to improve the town's architecture, notably by building the Sultan's palace, the Dar al Makhzen, within the fortified walls put up by the Almohads.

At the end of the nineteenth century, the population of the town was enriched by a merchant and lettered class who held posts in the *makhzen*, giving the town a genuine cultural and artistic life. As a result, Rabat is one of the very few towns in Morocco to have been both a *hadariya*, or centre of civilisation, and a political capital. In 1912, after the signing of the treaty establishing the French protectorate, General Lyautey, France's first resident general, moved the seat of his residence from Fez to Rabat, whose 20,000 inhabitants made it one of the most important towns in the country. With a royal residence and a merchant middle-class made up of former civil-servants of the *makhzen* and old Andalusian families it now became the capital of Morocco, though the title refers solely to administrative matters, not to economic or cultural affairs.

Today, the old medina – that Lyautey had no wish to change, for he was eager to preserve the cultural and social integrity of Morocco – sits side by side with the European quarter with its large, spacious complexes, wide avenues and green spaces. Together, they form a very pleasant city which has also been entrusted with a powerful symbol: since 1971, it contains the mausoleum of Mohammed V, the grandfather of the present king and the champion of Moroccan independence.

Rabat the White

Rabat-l'Ancienne is made up of three distinct entities: the medina and the Kasbah of the Oudaya, which are inside the Almohad walls, and, outside the walls, some two kilometres from the town-centre, the Merinid necropolis of Chella. Up until the turn of the century, the medina was limited to that part of it built by the Mudejars from Spain. In the huge Ribat al Fath, only the Hassan Tower, the royal palace and a few *agdal* (kitchen gardens and orchards) occupied the area today totally overrun by the modern city.

The walls surrounding the medina were for the most part built during the reign of Yakoub al Mansour (1184-1199). Five kilometres long, they protect the town to the west and the south, the other sides bene-fiting from the natural shelter afforded by cliff, river and ocean. A sturdy mixture of brick, stones and lime, they have stood up well to the erosions of time, and their orange-red patina gives Rabat its distinctive appearance. Ten metres high, they are crowned by a rampart walk and a parapet with merlons and flanked by numerous towers. On the side overlooking the river, the Alouites reinforced their defensive character by adding a second, four-meter-high wall built from quarry stones, throwing in a few bastions for good measure.

The most admired rampart in Rabat, however, is the Wall of the Mudejars (Andalous Ramparts), which runs in a straight line for more than 1,400 metres along the south of the town. Some five metres high, the wall is pierced with several Almohad gateways, amongst which Bab al Alou and Bab al Hadd, which the Andalusians fitted out with openings for canons. The Kasbah of the Oudaya, which rises up from the cliff opposite the medina, is a fully-fledged fortress named after the celebrated tribe installed there by Moulay Ismaïl to watch over the bellicose Arab Zaaer tribe plotting to overthrow the town. Separated from the medina by the square where the Al Ghazal Souk is held, it is staunchly defended by walls built largely by the Almohads in the twelfth century, then modified and restored in the seventeenth and eighteenth centuries by the Mudejars and the Alouite sovereigns. Its extremely irregular outline is a crucial part of its imposing military architecture. Of the wall overlooking the river only a few fragments remain, but the inland sections and those overlooking the sea are well preserved.

The Mudejars, meanwhile, fearing reprisals by land or sea, built the Pirates' Tower, the inner staircase of which leads down to the river. They also dug a complex network of underground passages leading to the other side of the kasbah and enlarged the window recesses of the old Almohad towers to accommodate canons.

The Alouite sovereign Moulay Rachid extended the ramparts in a south-easterly direction; today, they house the Museum of the Oudaya and the Andalusian garden. The surrounding walls of the kasbah had undeniable military value, forming a well-protected lair and a forward position from which the inhabitants could watch over and defend the town.

The medina can be reached through any one of six exceptionally well-preserved gateways built by the Almohads in the twelfth century. Four of these–Bab al Alou, Bab al Hadd, Bab al Rouah and the last, which has no name and is set into what is now the royal palace–open onto the longest side of the western wall, while only one, Bab al Zaaer, is to be found in the southern wall. The kasbah, meanwhile, boasts the most sumptuous of them all, Bab al Oudaya.

Bab al Alou, Bab al Hadd, Bab al Zaaer and the gateway to the royal palace have a number of architectural features in common. Four-stepped structures flanked on the outside by two projecting towers, they enclose a series of rectangular rooms between the antechambers of the entranceway and the exit. They also have an uncovered hallway and a number of small fitted rooms designed to accommodate soldiers on guard duty, shops and lodgings. Each gateway forms an imposing block that juts out into the surroundings on either side of the wall. The gateways constituted a highly effective defence system. Assailants had to force down the outside doors, then make their way along the stepped

BAB AL ROUAH

"The gate of the wind" is pierced in the western
wall of the city. More sober but every bit
as impressive as the gateway to the kasbah,
it today houses an art gallery. The upper area
of the embrasure of the gate has been
filled in with bricks to prevent
enemy cavalry from breaking through.

corridor and a series of rooms before arriving in the uncovered hall,
where they would immediately be vulnerable to missiles thrown by the
besieged.

The openings on the two sides are carefully made: large pointed horseshoe arches of cut stone with plain monochrome decorations. They are
adorned with *relievo voussoirs* and foiled circles carved into the stone.
The rigour and harmony of their proportions links them directly to the
Hispano-Mauresque architecture of the great empires.

Bab al Rouah ("the gate of the wind") differs from the other gateways in
being more monumental and more lavishly adorned. Its monumental
arch, flanked by two towers, is inserted in a massive, rectangular building with a buff-coloured facade. Surrounding the central arch are two
decorative arches carved with semi-circular and pointed lobes that trace
the main lines of the construction, giving it the rugged majesty one
would expect of a fortification. Each of the spandrels is carved with a
palm-leaf motif and subtly interlacing single or double wreathed palm
stalks, and framed by a calligraphic frieze.

Bab al Oudaya, which leads into the kasbah, looks down over the cliffs
of Bou Regreg and the medina of Rabat. Built by Yakoub al Mansour on

BAB AL OUDAYA

Attributed to Yakoub al Mansour, this gateway in cut stone gives access to the kasbah and is a masterpiece of Almohad architecture. Its horseshoe arch is framed by decorative festooned arches supported at their base by snakelike forms unusual in Moslem art.

Almohad lines, it presents a number of interesting architectural and aesthetic variations. Like all palace gateways in the Moslem world, it was also used as a guardroom and tribunal. Its has less military value, however, than the other gateways of the Ribat al Fath. The facade consists of a bay surrounded by a horseshoe arch and is flanked by two towers. All the builders' attention has been concentrated on the ornamentation, carved directly in the stone on both sides of the wall. The relief decoration is rich and varied, breaking down the whole of the upper surface into several tiered planes which trail off at the bottom edge of the parapet. The plain opening is built with ordinary arch-stones, whereas the semicircular arch surrounding it alternates rounded and pointed lobes made up of two overlapping braids. This in turn is framed by two stringcourses deeply carved with lozenge-shaped arabesques surrounded by stalk and palm-leaf motifs and surmounted by a calligraphic frieze. The remarkable decorative mastery of this work, where harmony is achieved without cluttering the surfaces, contrasts with the simplicity of the buildings in the Kasbah of the Oudaya and the medina.

The medina was built by the Mudejars in the seventeenth century and has a regular plan that is uncommon in Moroccan medinas. Houses and districts are spread over some 150 acres of land according to a rough

DECORATIVE DETAILS

Of all the imperial cities it is in Rabat
that the influence of Andalusian architecture
is most pronounced. Twice in its history,
in 1492 and 1610, it was home to a large
Mudejar community. Mural ornamentation
such as the stylised conch and the epigraphic
medallion are taken directly from Spain.

Pages 168 - 169 |

THE KASBAH OF THE OUDAYA
The whorled, decorative iron-work used
for the windows and doors
of middle-class homes is likewise
characteristic of Andalusian art.

grid-plan that was probably modelled on Spanish towns. Two roads running north-south and three major roads running east-west and aligned with the *qibla* control traffic. Narrow streets and blind alleys are grafted onto this main grid without turning the town into a maze, as so often happens with medinas. Rabat is not governed by the usual centralized logic, the Great Mosque and the souks for precious goods being laid out all the way along the Rue Suiqa ("little souk") in the south, somewhat off-centre in relation to the topographic heart. A great many trades have set up shop at the city gates, as have certain *kissariya* (Mouline) and *fondouks* (Ben Aïsha, Daouïa).

Though the Mudejars did not put up any monumental buildings inside the rampart walls, they exercised a lasting influence on the architecture and craftsmanship of the town. Certain forms, such as the semicircular or basket-handle arch, bear the Spanish stamp, as do ornamental designs like the pilaster composed of mouldings piled up over the top areas of doors and the wrought iron used in conjunction with windows and doors. The plain small houses huddled together in the medina are usually built with stone and whitewashed with lime, and are typical of seventeenth- and eighteenth-century Mudejar dwellings. Most of the

THE MEDINA

The roofs of sanctuaries stand out among the tightly-knit mass of terraced roofs. Mudejar doors are characterised by semicircular arches and coloured mouldings inspired by the Spanish Renaissance.

more monied homes are tucked away among the more humble dwellings of the district and are similar, in structure at least, to those of all Moroccan medinas; nevertheless, though built around patios, they are remarkable for their sobriety and discretion. The Kasbah of the Oudaya also contains, in addition to the palace and the Al Atiq Mosque, a district made up of simple dwellings reserved for *guich* (soldiers), most of them built in the early seventeenth century. One's overall impression of the medina is of a cat's-cradle of narrow streets and alleys lined with high, whitewashed walls.

Alongside these modest buildings, that are not without a certain charm, can be seen some of the most accomplished monumental architecture in the country. Though it was only at the turn of the century that Rabat acquired its official status as imperial capital, a fair measure of attention was paid to it by each dynasty in turn – and, in particular by the Almohad and Alouite sovereigns, who, as patrons of the arts, encouraged aesthetic reflection and magnificence in the arts.

THE HASSAN TOWER

The marble-pillared esplanade and the massive
tower overlooking the sea are all that remain
of the vast building project launched by Yakoub
al Mansour in the twelfth century.
The Almohad sovereign wanted to build
here a gigantic mosque where his entire
army could come together in prayer.

THE HASSAN TOWER

This majestic, unfinished minaret
has some of the soberness
of the Giralda in Seville
or the Koutoubiya in Marrakesh.
Each of its stone-carved walls
is decorated differently.

The Hassan Tower and the Great Mosques

At the turn of the century, the city of Rabat numbered some fifty
mosques, most of them built by Alouite sovereigns. Of various sizes,
they are generally laid out along traditional lines: a closed courtyard
sometimes surrounded by porticoes, a prayer-room, a *mihrab* and a
minaret. Successive alterations have in some cases spoiled their coherence by upsetting the original balance; nevertheless, the mosques of
Rabat are one of the capital's main architectural attractions, a symbol of
the religious fervour that for centuries fuelled the Moslem holy war.
The oldest sanctuary in Rabat, the Jamaa al Atiq Mosque, is situated in
the Kasbah of the Oudaya. Its foundations were laid in 1150 by the
Almohad sovereign Abd el Moumen. The mosque is still used as a place
of worship, and, at the turn of the century, the sultan sometimes came
here in person to perform his prayers. Restoration-work and alterations
were carried out at various points in its history, the most significant of
these being made in the eighteenth century during the reign of Moulay
Abdellah by the English renegade Ahmed al Inglizi. All that remains of
the original monument are the outside walls and one or two pillars in
the prayer-room. The asymmetrical plan, the unusual siting of the
minaret (placed behind the wall of the *qibla*) and the unaligned *mihrab*
are in marked contrast with the more distinguished examples of
Almohad religious architecture.

THE AL SOUNNA MOSQUE
Built by the Alouites in the eighteenth century opposite
the royal palace and heavily restored by King Hassan II,
the Al Sounna Mosque looks ahead
to the neo-Mauresque style favoured
by the architects of Louis Hubert Lyautey.

The Hassan Mosque of Rabat, on the other hand, is without contest one of the jewels passed down by that dynasty. Today, all that remains of that monumental undertaking are a few gigantic columns and a magnificent minaret, the Hassan Tower. Together with the new mausoleum of Mohammed V, the remains of the mosque dominate the hill overlooking Bou Regreg and are the main landmark of the city. The origin of *Hassan* (which means "goodness") remains mysterious: was it the name of a tribe, a place or a contractor? Work is thought to have been begun in 1196 under the aegis of the Almohad sovereign Yakoub al Mansour, whose death in 1199 left it unfinished. Building an edifice of this kind in the Middle Ages required the labour of several generations, as with the cathedrals of Europe. Over time, the materials used to build it were pillaged, and the earthquake of 1755 finally reduced it to a state of ruin. Its colossal scale and elaborate ornamentation suggest that the Almohad sovereign was planning to establish his new imperial capital in Rabat.
The Hassan Mosque, the esplanade of which today forms a huge rectangle, was intended to have been the largest religious edifice in the Moslem West; in the East, only the mosque of Samarra in Iraq was bigger. Its walls were pierced by fourteen gateways, and, on the north side of the building, a huge courtyard was laid out. Two further courtyards, on the east and west sides, were aligned with the bays, the central area being filled by the huge, pillared prayer-room.

THE AL SOUNNA MOSQUE
The minaret, pierced with gemel windows, is carved with arabesques over its upper area.
The central patio and two small, adjoining pavilions are used to perform one's ablutions.

The plan of the mosque perfectly illustrates the Almohad contractors' concern for balanced volumes: the minaret, prolonging the central axis, makes the lay-out absolutely symmetrical. Like all the mosques built by this dynasty, the oratory proper was T-shaped. Supported by rows of massive pillars, it was made up of eighteen bays and divided into twenty-one naves. Had it been completed in accordance with Almohad norms, the minaret would have measured 80 metres in height, making it taller than that of the Koutoubiya in Marrakesh. By the time of the sultan's death, only a very massive square tower (16 metres wide by 44 metres high) had been built. The interior, protected by walls more than two-and-a-half metres thick, is composed of six floors connected by a wide ramp giving access to the small, domed rooms. The four outside walls are carved with a filigree of blind arcades surmounted by a huge

network of intertwining geometrical designs, the mouldings overlapping in an arch-shaped honeycomb. While employing the same ornamental vocabulary, the composition varies from one wall to the next; the arches of the lower panels are sometimes pointed or horseshoe-shaped, sometimes foiled or decorated with stalactites.

The scale of the construction, with all the technical difficulties this will have involved, the elaborate architectural structure and the care taken over the ornamentation of the minaret testify to exceptional skill and give grounds to believe that the mosque was the work of the same architects who built the Koutoubiya in Marrakesh and the Giralda in Seville. This was the symbolic site on which Mohammed V, on his return from exile after the proclamation of independence in 1956, conducted the first solemn Friday prayers.

On the south side of the medina, near the Souk al Sebbat for shoes, is Jamaa al Kabir, called the Great Mosque. Built during the Merinid period in the thirteenth century, it has been subject to various modifications, notably during the reign of Moulay Sliman in the nineteenth century. The second largest mosque in Rabat after Jamaa al Sounna, its T-shaped oratory takes up ten naves and seven bays.

The Al Sounna Mosque, built in the eighteenth century by Sidi Mohammed ben Abdellah, occupies a strategic position in the modern town at the northernmost point of the walls of the Touargas. Its handsome minaret, visible from afar, looks proudly down on Rabat. Finally, among many others, the sanctuary of Moulay Sliman, Jamaa al Suiqa, situated in the medina's souk district and rebuilt in 1812, is one of those cathedral-mosques of which Rabat is justly proud.

PALACE OF THE KASBAH OF THE OUDAYA

Unlike the other imperial capitals, Rabat had no royal residence until the time of the Alouites. Built between 1672 and 1694, the palace of the kasbah of the Oudaya was the home of Moulay Ismaïl's son.

PALACE OF THE KASBAH OF THE OUDAYA

The four buildings containing the living quarters were organized around a porticoed courtyard decorated with a fountain. The palace also had a mosque, a *hammam* and an angle-tower that is well preserved.

Pages 178-179

PALACE OF THE KASBAH OF THE OUDAYA

The original ornamentation of the palace,
which is now a museum of traditional arts,
has been preserved–in this case,
a mural composition of *zillij* arranged
around sixteen-pointed stars.
The builders of this princely residence
were above all concerned
with sobriety and balance.

Between the early death of Yakoub al Mansour and the coming of the Alouite dynasty, there was no royal residence in Rabat. The first Alouite sovereigns to stop over in the city lived in small palaces built on the south-west side of the Ribat al Fath, inside the Almohad walls; only one of these palaces was in the kasbah. The kasbah, then, did not house the traditional palace complex of the king that gives the other great royal cities their prestige.

The palace of the Kasbah of the Oudaya, where the Alouite sovereigns lived when they stayed in Rabat, dates from the reign of Moulay Ismaïl. On the wooden lintels of the central patio you can read: "Abiding happiness and brilliant victory to our lord Ismaïl, Commander of the faithful". According to Moroccan tradition, it was the son and successor of that king, Prince Moulay Mohammed al Dehbi, who supervised the construction of this building between 1672 and 1694. The history of the palace is still not properly known. It is known to have been fully restored and slightly modified in 1917, under the Protectorate, and to have undergone further alterations in the course of the century. It currently houses the Rabat Museum of Traditional Arts.

The palace was built along the lines of the traditional Moroccan city dwelling, while the stepped main entrance likewise respects the structure of traditional gateways. The residence consists of a main building organized around a courtyard decorated with a white marble pond and surrounded by large rectangular rooms adorned with marble flagstones and geometrical coffered ceilings. Within can be found the reconstruction of a traditional Moroccan interior: pottery from Fez, mats, illuminated manuscripts, pieces of embroidery, costumes, musical instruments and Berber jewellery.

A beautiful rectangular garden in the Andalusian style is laid out on the south side of the palace, conferring on it the status of a princely residence. This enormous orchard is composed of stone-curbed ponds, tiered esplanades and paved paths that separate clumps of shrubs, gaily laid-out multicoloured flowers and a prodigious wealth of trees which give to the whole a feeling of well-being and rest. On the ramparts nearby is the Moorish cafe, which affords a splendid view of the Bou Regreg. The museum-palace of the Oudaya was never used as a main residence by any of the Alouite sovereigns.

The Dar al Bhar Palace is the work of Moulay Sliman, who built it between 1792 and 1799 facing the ocean. Right up to the turn of the century, sultans were still coming here with members of the royal family to get away from court life. Moulay Abdelaziz, who received General Lyautey and various French dignitaries here in 1907, undertook major extensions that were never completed. Dar al Bhar was gradually abandoned, and today all but a handful of its buildings have disappeared. Only a pavilion, left relatively untouched, has been integrated with a group of buildings designed to accommodate a military hospital.

**GARDEN OF THE KASBAH
OF THE OUDAYA**

At the turn of the century, a garden
planted with flowers and fruit
trees was added to the palace.

THE ROYAL PALACE
This magnificent
succession of
entranceways leads
to the heart of Dar
al Makhzen where
some two thousand
people live.

THE GATE "OF THE AMBASSADORS"

This elegant network of multifoiled arcs
supported by white colonnettes displays
the traditional structure of the *chebka*,
a form of ornamentation typical of Almohad art.

The Royal Palace is the current residence of the King of Morocco. Now that it houses this royal city and all its monuments, Rabat can at last hold its own against its elders, Fez and Marrakesh. It can also advance, as an argument in its favour, the sacred character that has helped shape its history and its landscape. Dar al Makhzen, which dates from 1864, was constructed on the ruins of the royal palace built in the late eighteenth century by Sidi Mohammed ben Abdellah. Today, more than two thousand people inhabit this architectural complex which extends over a vast esplanade (the *mechouar*) surrounded by its own private walls. In it can be found the residence of government (the palace proper), a mosque, barracks for the royal guard, a royal college, a small race-track and a variety of ministerial buildings dotted about its enormous and well-tended gardens.

Like so many royal palaces in Morocco, the organization of this modern palace clearly reflects the traditional lay-out of Hispano-Mauresque palace complexes; in its division into three distinct but interconnecting parts, for example. The first of these is the *mechouar*, the part open to the public, where important visitors are welcomed and where the sovereign receives his subjects for the *bayaa*, a sort of oath of allegiance under

THE FEAST OF THE THRONE

The Feast of the Throne brings together the hooded white silhouettes of hundreds of notables from throughout the country, come to pay allegiance to His Majesty the King Hassan II and celebrate in this way the stability of the kingdom.

which senior civil servants of the State recognise the authority of the king. Next comes the throne room with the *diwan*, a reception area that is the most richly decorated and monumental area in the entire building. And, finally, there is the harem, living quarters that are usually built around patios and *riyads* and which constitute the private living-space of the royal family.

Constructed along the same lines as traditional city dwellings, all these buildings are covered with saddlebacked or double saddlebacked green-tiled roofs and look out onto vast and richly ornamented gardens and courtyards. Set round with finely carved pleasure pavilions (*menzeh*) fronted by wide galleries and loggias, the gardens consist of a network of raised, *zillij*-paved paths that intersect at right angles and are separated by flower beds. Basins of Roman- or Andalusian-style ribbed marble stand in ponds inlaid with polychrome glazed tiling. One royal apartment and green space after another is organized around these cool courtyards where a complex play of shadow and light holds a shifting mirror up to the subtle geometrical forms of the *zillij*. Outside, the palace opens onto an immense park planted with different varieties of trees and large flower-beds.

The Mohammed V mausoleum, the most recent and the most majestic of the Alouite monuments of Rabat, likewise testifies to royal splendour, in particular to the cult surrounding the father of independence. Born in Fez in 1909, Mohammed V succeeded his father Moulay Youssef to the throne in 1927. In a speech delivered in Tangier in 1947, he called for national sovereignty for his country. Deposed by French troops and exiled to Madagascar in 1953, he was called back to the throne two years later. In 1956, he obtained independence for his country, reigning over it until his death in 1961. Consecrated and greatly respected by his people, it wasn't until 1971 that he was actually interred in the mausoleum. Ten years were needed to build opposite the Hassan Tower and overlooking the Bou Regreg this edifice whose astonishing classicism is in the best imperial tradition.

Placed on a three-and-a-half-metre-high base built of white Italian marble, the monument is crowned with a pyramid-shaped roof covered with green tiles. Access is by way of a wrought-iron gate and a staircase leading up to the cupola that shelters the sarcophagus. The four sides of the marble cube forming the body of the building are each pierced by three entrances in the form of multifoiled arches, the one in the middle being larger than the other two. From a balcony you can admire the sarcophagus, which is carved from a block of white onyx from Pakistan placed on a slab of granite so highly polished that the sepulchre might almost be floating on a pond. The gigantic chandelier that hangs from the ceiling of the dome is the work of Fassi craftsmen. In a corner of the mausoleum is the marble tomb of Prince Moulay Abdellah, who died in 1983. The ornamentation, the work of the finest craftsmen in Morocco, is in keeping with the tradition of royal mausoleums: a dome decorated with painted stalactites, calligraphic friezes in Maghebi script, string-courses of chiselled and gilded plaster, polychrome *zillij* and white marble colonnettes. The siting of the mausoleum, opposite the Hassan Tower and the unadorned columns of the ghost of the Great Mosque, only adds to the solemnity of the building: here, facing each other in silence, two sovereigns whose acts were to prove decisive for their country set their seal on eight centuries of Moroccan history.

Chella, the Merinid Necropolis

Rising up over the south bank of the Bou Regreg, a few kilometres upstream from the estuary and not far from the southern rampart of Rabat, in a fertile valley where clear water flows in abundance, are the ruins of the Roman town of Sala, a name which probably meant "the Rocks" in Punic. In the Islamic period, this ancient settlement was drained of its inhabitants when the medina of Salé was founded on the opposite bank of the river, near the sea. The name itself, then, must have been transferred to the new town, the vestiges of the abandoned city being called Chella.

How did these ruins become, in the late thirteenth century, the necropolis of the Merinids? We should first of all bear in mind that the military actions undertaken by the sovereigns of that dynasty against the Catholic kings of Spain led to their often frequenting, like their Almohad predecessors, the holy site of Ribat al Fath. To understand why the Merinids invested these ruins with this new funerary role, however, one needs to remember their commitment to the holy war and their attachment to this rallying point for "fighters of the faith".

It was the first caliph of this dynasty, Abou Youssef Yakoub, who chose this precise spot as a retreat, a place in which to think things over and meditate. He had a mosque built there amid the ruins of the old Roman town and buried his wife, Oum al Izzen, there in 1284. After his death in Algesiras in 1286, he was buried there in his turn. He was laid to rest in the westernmost of the two mosques of the funeral complex, as were his two successors, Abou Yakoub (died 1307) and Abou Thabit (died 1308). The Merinid sovereigns' attachment to the necropolis is intimate-ly bound up with the holy war: whenever they abandoned the

THE NECROPOLIS OF CHELLA

Built outside the Almohad ramparts
on the Roman site of Sala,
the thirteenth-century Merinid necropolis
concealed behind these imposing
walls is a delightful and very peaceful spot.

THE ZAOUIYA OF CHELLA

The ruins of this sanctuary built
by Abou al Hassan are today overrun
with vegetation. Some of the polychrome
faience ornamentation of its handsome
minaret remains, while storks have
built their nests at the top of its turret.

THE ENTRANCE TO THE NECROPOLIS

One of the most beautiful of Merinid military gateways, its richly decorated horseshoe archis framed by two powerful towers.

affairs of Andalusia, their interest in the necropolis declined and they neglected what for their ancestors was an act of piety. Chella was thus subject to periods of neglect and to periods of sustained attention. Nevertheless, the sultan Abou Saïd (1300-1331) and his son Abou al Hassan (1331-1351) once more took up the traditions of the early princes of the dynasty, investing the necropolis with the ceremonial splendour it deserved. The second of the two sultans, in particular, remembered the sepulchres of his forbears and decided, at the height of his power–when he had taken possession of Tunis, making him master of all North Africa–to build a full-scale funeral complex.

Using the ochre-coloured stones of Rabat he built powerful walls that still surround the city to this day. To do this, he would probably have had to heighten the old Roman ramparts. Built on undulating terrain, these six-to-ten-meter-high, crenellated walls are shaped like an irregular polygon.

The rampart walk is reinforced by twenty square towers, likewise crenellated, which stand out in relief from the walls at more or less regular intervals. Three gateways give access within. The main entrance to this city of the dead and refuge for the faithful, however, can be found on the

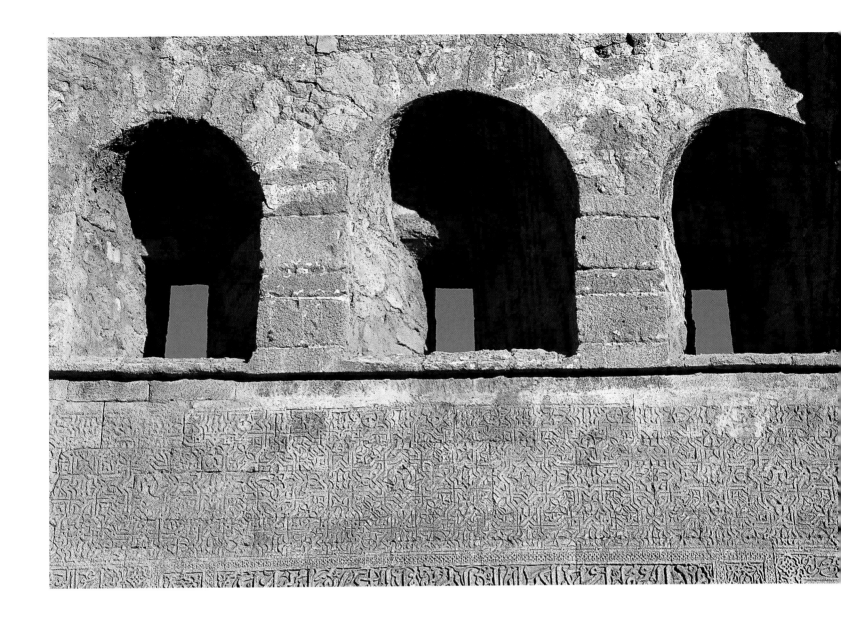

west side and is at once more monumental and more richly carved. The powerful bay is flanked by two octagonal towers surmounted by square balconies set round with merlons at each of their four corners and supported by corbellings decorated with stalactites. The opening, in the shape of a horseshoe arch, is set into a rectangular stone facade and is similar to those of the Almohad gateways on which it is modelled. The ornamentation, however, which is carved directly into the stone and has the delicacy of chiselled plaster, spills over onto the upper areas of the towers, making the gateway one of the most interesting examples of Merinid military architecture. The sovereigns of that dynasty lavished the same ceremonial splendour and the same skill on all their monuments, whether civil or religious. The pointed arch of the gateway is surrounded by two further arches and crowned with an epigraphic frieze giving the name of the man who built this rampart in 1339, Abou al Hassan; above this is a richly decorated second frieze supported by white marble columns resting on blue marble corbels. With its spandrels richly carved with interlacing plant forms, a few touches of blue faience on its upper part to fix the light and its scalloped palm-leaf designs, the edifice, for all its sturdiness, is remarkably elegant, albeit lacking in

the majesty of Almohad gateways. The rear facade evokes even more emphatically their subtle aesthetic: strong and balanced.

As you come out from underneath its stepped arch, a small valley of surprising beauty meets your eye. The poetry of its green, flowering gardens irrigated by canals, where crystalline water gushes forth from a sacred spring, mingles with the charm of the ruins. Beyond its fields filled with slender reeds, cactus plants and trees, a group of ruined buildings rises up here and there from an olive grove, while in the distance a fairy-tale horizon opens up: the river, the marshes, the wide, grassy valley and hills shimmering like shot silk. Part of the land is occupied by the ruins of the Roman town, the rest is given over to the Merinid sanctuaries. Walking down the path, notice on your left the enormous courtyard surrounded by rooms once reserved for pilgrims, and, on your right, a four-cornered edifice built by the sultan for his guards. At the lowest point of the enclosure can be found the actual funeral complex of Abou al Hassan, which has its own surrounding wall and still contains on its south-west side the ruins of the mosque of Abou Youssef, his tomb and those of other members of the royal family, a *zaouiya* (that religious establishment which is part mosque, part teaching centre and part hostel for pilgrims and students), a few ruined galleries and shards of mosaic. Built by Abou al Hassan, the *zaouiya* was laid out and decorated in exactly the same manner as the *madrasas* of Fez and, according to some authors, was even more luxurious. The prophet Mohammed is said to have prayed in the oratory. In the old days, all you had to do to earn the title of *hadj*, normally reserved for pilgrims to Mecca, was to walk seven times round the tower of the *mihrab*. The minaret, which is badly damaged, was certainly one of the most beautiful of its day. Abou al Hassan rebuilt the upper part, embellishing it with a delicate filigree of black, white, green and blue *zillij*.

Today, it is a favourite nesting-place for storks. In the space left free inside the enclosure the sultan laid out a very elegant garden planted with orange and lemon trees and criss-crossed, like the *riyads* of Moroccan palaces, with small alleys paved with mosaics. It was here that he had his own mausoleum built, a masterpiece of carved stone and faience tiling that was originally surmounted by a dome which is now in ruins. Not far from the mausoleum is another edifice of the same shape, built to accommodate readers of the Koran and likewise in ruins. The stele of Abou al Hassan, the last sovereign to be buried there, is still in place amid the ruins of his mausoleum, as is that of his wife Chams al Doha ("the Morning Sun"), a Christian converted to Islam who died in 1349 and the mother of the great sovereign Abou Inan.

ORNAMENTATION OF THE GATEWAY OF THE CHELLA
An Almohad conch stands out against
delicately carved vegetal arabesques.
The festooned arches are supported by snakelike
designs carved directly in the stone.

ZAOUIYA OF CHELLA
Built around a courtyard were
a small oratory and cells for pilgrims.

The necropolis of Chella, famed throughout the entire Merinid reign, received illustrious visitors like the Andalusian poet and scholar Lisan al Din al Khatib. It was permanently abandoned at the end of the Merinid dynasty, however, and was pillaged several times over the centuries. In 1755, an earthquake accelerated its destruction. Nature ran wild, and hundreds of storks and other waders invested the site, building their nests on the minaret and on the tops of trees. There is something eerie about the place at dusk, with their deafening cries. The site has once more become a sanctuary. The Spring of the Canons, for example, awash with eels, is held sacred, since these fish are said to have the power to heal sterility. Women eager to conceive light votive candles along the water's edge, and the atmosphere is positively ghostly. Especially since other legends circulate about Chella, where the jinns of Moulay Yakoub stand guard over the treasure that the sovereign is thought to have buried there. A visitor blessed with *baraka* might one day find Solomon's ring, on which the duration of the Jewish empire depends and which lies shrouded in millennial sleep beneath the ruins of Chella.

MINARET OF THE ZAOUIYA
The minaret is beautifully decorated
with geometrical intertwining tracery
and fleurons with vertical-domed palmettes
incrusted with turquoise mosaic.

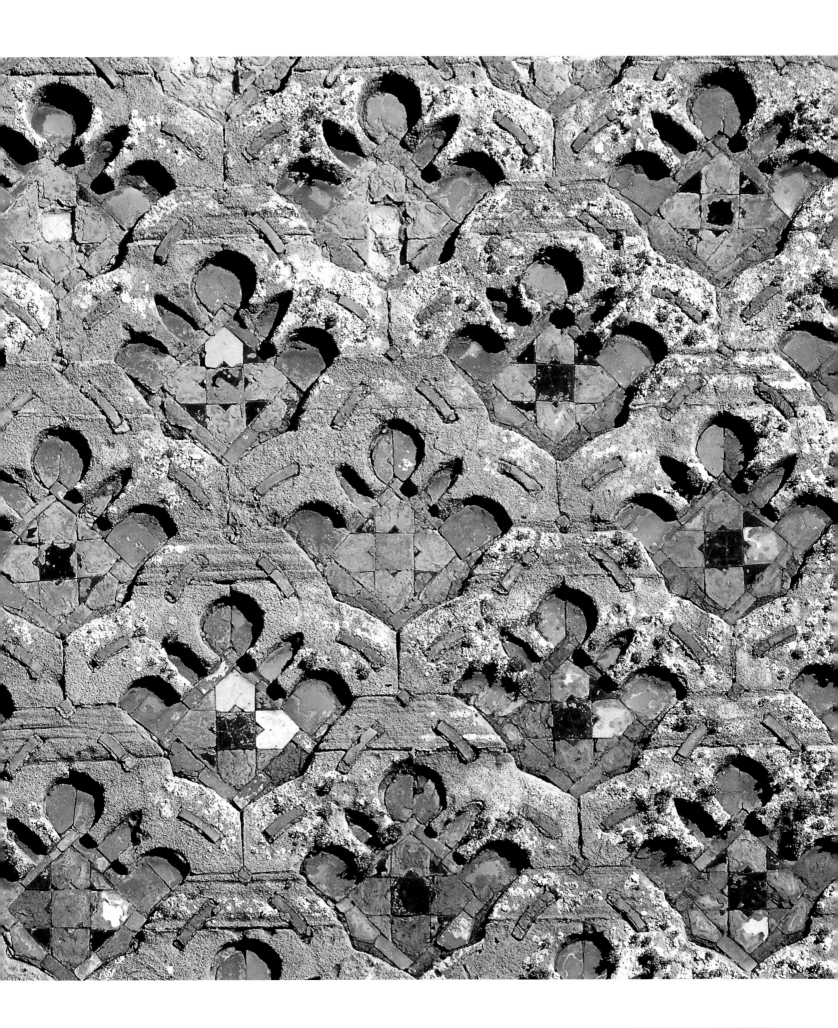

Appendices

Map of Morocco

Fez

GATEWAYS
1 - Bab al Chorfa
2 - Bab Guissa
3 - Bab al Ftouh
4 - Bab al Mahrouq

SANCTUARIES
5 - Al Karaouyin Mosque
6 - Andalous Mosque
7 - Al Tijani Zaouiya
8 - Moulay Idriss Zaouiya

PALACES
9 - Dar al Makhzen (Royal Palace)
10 - Dar al Batha
11 - Dar al Moqri

MADRASAS
12 - Bou Inania Madrasa
13 - Al Attarin Madrasa
14 - Al Sahrij Madrasa

OTHER MONUMENTS AND DISTRICTS
15 - Al Nejjarin Fondouk
16 - Tanners' Souk
17 - Mellah
18 - Kasbah of the Chrarda

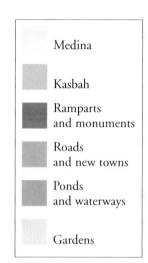

Medina

Kasbah

Ramparts and monuments

Roads and new towns

Ponds and waterways

Gardens

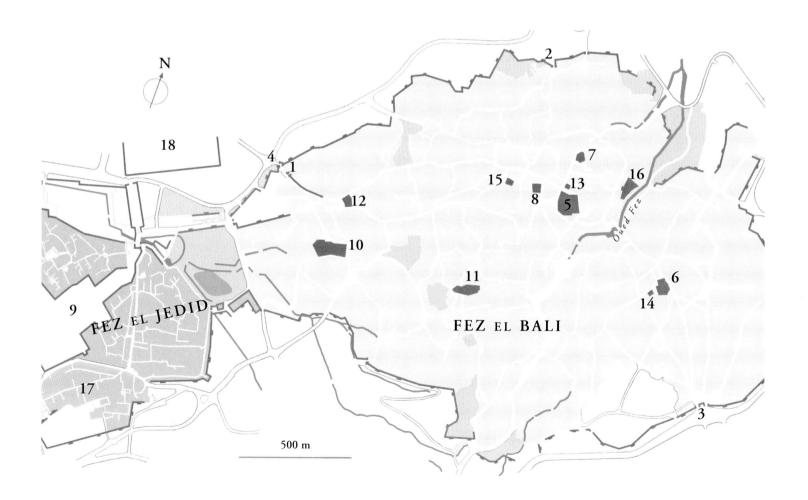

N

18

4
1

12

10

15
8

7

13
5

16

11

6

14

9

FEZ EL JEDID

FEZ EL BALI

Oued Fez

17

3

500 m

Marrakesh

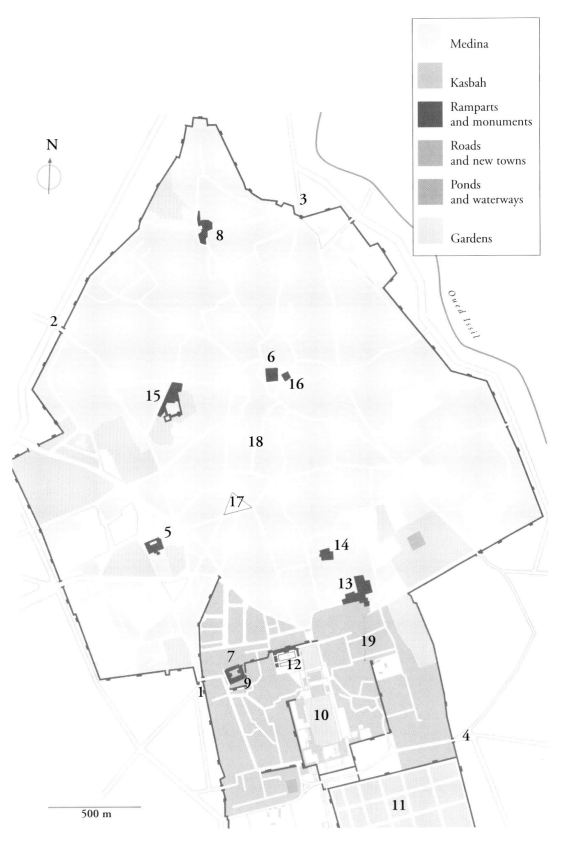

N

500 m

GATEWAYS
1 - Bab Agnaou
2 - Bab Doukkala
3 - Bab al Khemis
4 - Bab al Hmar

SANCTUARIES
5 - The Koutoubiya
6 - Ben Youssef Mosque
7 - Kasbah Mosque
8 - Sidi bel Abbes Mausoleum
9 - Mausoleum
of the Saadian Princes

PALACES AND GARDENS
10 - Dar al Makhzen
(Royal Palace)
11 - Agdal Gardens
12 - Al Badi Palace
13 - Al Bahia palace
14 - Dar Si Saïd
15 - Dar al Glaoui

**OTHER MONUMENTS
AND DISTRICTS**
16 - Ben Youssef Madrasa
17 - Place Jamaa al Fna
18 - Souks
19 - Mellah

Medina

Kasbah

Ramparts
and monuments

Roads
and new towns

Ponds
and waterways

Gardens

Oued Issil